THE VOLUNTEER COMMUNITY
creative use of human resources
SECOND EDITION

Eva Schindler-Rainman

*Organizational Consultant to Voluntary
and Governmental Organizations*

Ronald Lippitt

*Professor Emeritus, University of Michigan
President, Human Resource Development Associates*

University Associates, Inc.
8517 Production Avenue
P.O. Box 26240
San Diego, California 92126

A FANTASY

*Written for and presented to The Volunteers Personnel Committee
of the Young Women's Christian Association of New York City, 1952*

In recent years, as I have pondered over the vicissitudes of
Democracy, it has often occurred to me to wonder what would
happen if, in the United States, all citizens who work for nothing,
who serve as volunteers, were suddenly to "go on strike."

This band of strikers would include all trustees of colleges,
universities and private schools; all members of local school
boards; all directors of private institutions and agencies; all
solicitors for community chests; all lay boards collaborating with
public institutions and agencies, all committee members of private
institutions and agencies; and that great host of citizens who
serve multitudes of educational, welfare, health and recreational
organizations in one capacity or another. How large would the
total be? I know of no reliable count but the total would certainly
fall in the neighborhood of twenty-five to thirty million persons.

What would happen if this corps of citizens who labor without
pay, who exercise their own free will in choosing the functions
they will perform, were to resign their posts, refuse to attend
meetings, to disengage themselves from all responsibilities?

It is difficult to imagine what American life minus its
volunteers would be like, but one may make a few assumptions.

Officials and professionals would, no doubt, continue to
operate their respective institutions and agencies, at least for
a time, but they would function in a lonely atmosphere. They
would find themselves insulated from the true public and in touch
with only that sector of the public which is represented by their
constituents and clients. There would no longer be a life-line
between their expertness and the experience of the people.
The transmission belt which shuttles back and forth between
Democracy on the one hand and Science on the other would
stand idle. They, the professionals, would soon be obliged to
devote large amounts of time and energy in securing funds
for the maintenance of their work and assurance for their
incomes. Public agencies would take on more and more of the
coloration of bureaucracies. Private agencies would, I believe,
gradually wither and die. And when private institutions no
longer exist Democracy will have committed suicide. Totalitarian

bureaucracies or dictatorships will take its place and freedom will disappear altogether.

I wish I knew how to induce volunteers to appreciate the significant role they play in furnishing vitality to the democratic enterprise. They are to Democracy what circulation of the blood is to the organism. They keep Democracy alive. They epitomize freedom and are to our society what the Bill of Rights is to the Constitution which governs us. The health of a democratic society may be measured in terms of the quality of services rendered by citizens who act in "obedience to the unenforceable"

The above phrase "obedience to the unenforceable" was used in a memorable address delivered by Lord Moulton before the Authors' Club of London and later published in the Atlantic Monthly. We live, said Lord Moulton, under the discipline of three domains: one, the positive law which prescribes rules of conduct and exacts penalties for disobedience; two, the realm of free choice which is covered by no statutes; and three, that domain in which neither positive law nor free choice prevails. In this sphere the individual imposes obligations upon himself. In this realm the individual is not wholly free, since he has accepted a responsibility. Although he knows that no law and no individual may compel him to fulfill this commitment, he also knows that he cannot disobey without betraying himself. This is the domain in which the volunteer lives, and as Lord Moulton concluded "the real greatness of a nation, its true civilization, is measured by the extent of this land of obedience to the unenforceable".

Eduard C. Lindeman

INTRODUCTION

Introduction

It seems appropriate at a time of massive changes, a time of transition, a time of new opportunities and confrontations to bring out a new edition of **THE VOLUNTEER COMMUNITY.** This volume is the result of our studies, reflections and involvements in the Volunteer World both here and abroad. We hope it will be a useful resource, stimulus, and guide for staffs and volunteers in public and private agencies offering volunteers an opportunity to serve; for the organizers and leaders of cause movements; for consultants doing organizational development work with agency decision makers: for professors in professional schools and sequences such as social work, health, medicine, psychology, psychiatry, nursing, religion, public administration, etc.; for leaders in business and labor; and for anyone interested in voluntarism as a vital part of an active democratic society.

The profile of the current volunteer has changed recently in the United States. The volunteer may be any person, female or male, from a wide age range from young to older, from all ethnic, religious and racial groups, from a variety of life styles, economic, educational, and social backgrounds, working without monetary compensation for their services in a cause or job they have voluntarily chosen. Their motivation will vary from wanting to make a difference to enter the paid job market. Many volunteers now receive enabling moneys for meals, transportation, baby sitting, conference registration, as well as being covered by insurance while on the volunteer job.

We feel it is important to clarify your expectations, to define the ways in which this volume may be helpful and the areas in which it should not be expected to be the appropriate resource. For example:

- It cannot transmit "how-to-do-it" skills, but it can identify and clarify needed skills of innovative leadership, trainership, and administration of volunteer activity.
- It cannot provide the specifics of program design and activity, but it can give you ideas and models and suggest guidelines for adaptation to your own specific needs.

- It cannot provide the objectives of your particular program.
- It cannot provide you with the materials you need for recruiting, orientation, and training activities, but it will help you define needed training materials and will suggest approaches to producing or locating them and using them effectively.
- It does not attempt to present a social criticism or commentary on the major issues, confrontations, and value orientations in the field of voluntarism, nor does it present a general sociological theory about voluntarism, but it should help you develop a philosophical base for clarifying your own priorities in the leadership and development of volunteer programs.
- It characterizes the development and functioning of voluntarism as a key aspect of a democratic society, but it does not take the position that all voluntarism is good.
- It attempts to link you to new practices and emerging ideas about voluntarism, to perspectives about the future of voluntarism, to the literature about voluntarism and to other resources in the field.

Let's preview briefly the flow of our presentation. We begin in Chapter I with some assumptions about the relationship between democracy, voluntarism, and personal growth and development. We focus on the major tasks that must be confronted and creatively coped with by a democratic system, national or local. We look at ways in which there can be effective mobilization and use of volunteer time, energy, and wisdom to create and maintain an effective self-renewing society, community, agency, or small group.

In Chapter II we summarize social trends that we think will have major relevance for the development of voluntarism. Chapter III contains an analysis of the variety of needs and opportunities for volunteers in every community and a review of some of the major new patterns and trends in the opportunities for volunteers. In Chapter IV we explore the bases of motivation of those who volunteer, and we challenge professionals to extend their use of and trust in volunteers. Chapter V summarizes and analyzes the problems and practices of recruitment and orientation of volunteers, examining some of the new approaches to the involvement of traditionally underutilized volunteer manpower. In Chapter IV we explore goals, methods, and designs for the preservice and in-service training of volunteers. In Chapter VII we focus on the need for the training of trainers of volunteers, illustrating designs and activities for helping the professional to develop trainership skills and perspectives. Chapter VIII deals with the functions and roles of the administrator of volunteer programs. It includes some characteristics of humanely and well managed volunteer programs. Chapter IX is an illustrative, integrated example of a collaborative community effort, mobilizing leaders, staff, volunteers and other community citizens to improve their quality of life. We present in Chapter X a "case study of the future," describing what a community might look like in action when the resources and motivations of the great variety of potential volunteers are fully utilized for the growth of the community and for the personal dèvelopment of individual citizens.

In a concluding Epilogue we attempt to help you make a bridge between this volume and your own back-home operating situations, suggesting resources and methods you might use to implement any ideas you may have developed for experimentation and innovation. The Epilogue is followed by a comprehensive, classified, annotated bibliography of a significant selection of the available literature about voluntarism and volunteering.

When we began this project, there was a critical need for scanning, reviewing, and evaluating the area of voluntary activity, because of the many exciting changes in this field and because of the predictable explosion of interest and the development of new programs in line with major social trends and social needs. We also believed that with the growing base of social science and concept development, it would be very important to help link theory concept, theory, and value to the methods, strategies, and skills needed for success in the effective recruitment and utilization of volunteers. We wanted to share the excitement and optimism we have gained from our own wide variety of experiences in helping communities, organizations, and cause groups develop their use of volunteer human resources. We also hope to give you some linkage to the many innovative new practices being devised by creative leaders working with new volunteer populations.

At the same time, we felt we should examine the serious problems of lag or discrepancy between the growing number of spontaneous action organizations and the traditionally organized groups, and between unplanned, ineffective efforts and successful implementations. Goodwill and motivation to contribute to human service and social change are proliferating in many directions from many sources, but often these efforts die or achieve only minor influence because of inadequate perspectives, methods, and strategies. These unsuccessful experiences are harmful to the motivating fiber of democratic voluntarism.

As a consequence of sharing our thinking with you through this volume, we hope we may be able to initiate a continuing active dialogue with many of you, involving exchange of concepts, values, and practices.

We want to express our deep appreciation to Thea Key and Betty Huber for their help in the revision of this manuscript. Also we are indebted to many colleagues and friends for their stimulation, support and ideas which have been helpful in the revision. In many ways, of course, our greatest indebtedness is to the numerous organizations and agencies that have invited us to work with them in the development of their programs, have shared their feedback from their experiences with us, and have led us to an everdeepening appreciation of the vitality and creative resourcefulness that continually manifest themselves on the growing edge of our social system.

I Democracy and Voluntarism

Two basic premises about the relationship between democracy and voluntarism have guided us in the development of this volume:

- A democratic social system—nation, state, community, organization, or group—must depend to a high degree on the volunteered time and energy of its members for its maintenance, stability, growth, and development.
- A democratic social system provides the conditions for a personally satisfying, self-actualizing growth opportunity for each individual.

It is true that a variety of nondemocratic social systems have inspired volunteer commitment and energy and have cultivated the development of individual capacities, but the idea of the democratic system and the democratic person involves some specific value judgments about the desirable society and person and the desirable pattern of voluntarism. Therefore, we want to start by sharing our thoughts on the nature of democratic social systems and democratic personalities, and then link these ideas to the processes of volunteering which are the major focus of this volume.

The Structures and Procedures of Democratic Systems

To establish, maintain, and continually revise the social climate in which democratic processes can function and flourish requires a great deal of collaboration in the development of appropriate political, economic, legal, and organizational mechanisms and structures. Before we approach the need for voluntarism, it will help us to review those dimensions of a democratic system which seem to be required for the growth and maintenance of internal democratic processes and for effective external relations with interdependent systems of all types. Much of the background thinking in this chapter is derived from *Autocracy and Democracy,* a study by R. K. White and R. Lippitt.[1]

The Structures of Opportunities for Participation. The democratic social system must provide opportunities for the widespread and continuing participation of its members in appropriate levels of decision making, planning, and action taking. The opportunity structures include a great variety of relationships, formal and informal, horizontal and vertical, geographical, etc. The concept of "outreach effort" is a critical aspect of the idea of participation. Often, providing opportunity for participation means setting up a structure of representation, that is, delegating responsibility to certain members to represent the various subgroups that have different interests and resources and will be affected in different ways by decisions and actions.

Participation may be of various types, depending on the function of the group. In our national society there are opportunities for participation in economic, political, occupational, cultural, and recreational life. The concept of "appropriate levels of participation" includes the ideas that there be appropriate designs for participation at all age levels and that there be equality of inclusion and participation for individuals of all political orientations and all racial, ethnic, religious, and economic backgrounds.

Procedures for Coordination, Linkage, and Conflict Utilization. In a pluralistic and fragmented democratic social system, made up of many types of individuals and groups, a major requirement is that the system establish procedures to provide for full communication, for orderly confrontation and conflict resolution, and for the coordination and blending of the energies and interests of the disparate subgroups. These procedures must be a creative substitute for the imposed hierarchical controls of autocratic systems.

As we will see in Chapter II, dealing creatively with internal polarization is one of the most critical challenges in our society, with great implications for voluntarism. As Kenneth Benne once said, our American democratic system has done fairly well with two elements of the ideological framework of the French revolution, i.e., "liberté" and "égalité," but very poorly with the third,

[1] White, R. K., and Lippitt, R. *Autocracy and Democracy.* New York: Harper and Brothers, 1960.

"fraternité." [2] In other words, we have not done well with the mechanisms for relationships between the "peer systems" which make up our democratic system. The procedures for intergroup cooperation, conflict utilization, and competition in most cases have not been worked through to develop more creative solutions than the "win-lose" solution.

Procedures for Planning. The continuous and sensitive monitoring of the future, its dangers and potentialities, is a critical responsibility of a democratic system. It requires the assignment of specialized responsibilities to gather data about the trends of change, to develop knowledge about the future by projection and analysis, and to make this knowledge widely available for creative participation in planning.

Often some of the more unsophisticated and uninvolved members of our society are accused of being oriented to the "here-and-now" rather than to the future and its consequences. But they are unlikely to become future-oriented unless they are given a sense of potency, of being able to have some influence on the developing future and some stake in its consequences. Leaders of democratic systems must recognize this fact and help the less powerful and the less advantaged to have meaningful and successful experiences in planning ahead.

Structures and Procedures for Internal and External Diagnostic Fact Finding. Another crucial requirement for a democracy is to be continuously sensitive to its many participants' varying degrees of need, desire, and readiness for change. A democracy must also achieve comparable sensitivity about other systems with which it is interdependent.

Therefore, the commitment of budget, manpower, and energy to diagnostic fact finding is crucial for analyzing both the internal functioning of the democratic system and the external relations of the system to other systems. Study of previous experience which may deepen understanding of the present and future is an important part of the analysis task. The more varied the subgroups that make up the system and the more rapid the processes of internal and external change, the more crucial it is to invest heavily in diagnostic research.

It is unfortunate that in times of political or economic stress and

[2] Benne, Kenneth D. "The Uses of Fraternity." *Daedalus,* Spring 1961. pp. 233-46.

change, when diagnostic fact finding is most needed, this is often the first thing to be cut out of the budget. Such a shortsighted policy greatly reduces the capability of the system to cope innovatively with change, transition, and crisis. One of the difficulties is that the critical research aimed at improving democratic processes is often not seen by leadership to have yielded as significant a payoff as research aimed at mastering the biological and physical aspects of the environment.

Support for Trying Out New Patterns. The wide base of involvement in diagnosis and planning in a democracy also provides a wide base of innovation for converting awareness of problems into ideas for change. In every phase of our American life—education, social welfare, family life, health care, recreation, governmental affairs—there is potential for experimentation with new models of social organization and social relationship. In the field of biological engineering, amazing improvements of agricultural practices have been made because of the support of demonstration farms and experimental stations for developing and trying out new practices. The research and development programs of our industrial enterprises have brought about the same kinds of miracles in improving physical technology. It is even more critical for a democracy's development and survival that it stimulate and support research and development in the improvement of the social processes.

Networks for the Dissemination of New Resources. The basic democratic idea of fairness, or equality of opportunity, suggests that when a new resource for the betterment of living is discovered, there is a commitment to disseminating this resource as rapidly and as widely as possible. Our national social system is remarkably backward in the development of mechanisms for disseminating the rapid accumulation of social inventions for a better life, such as new parental practices, new classroom teaching designs, new social work and health education skills, and new approaches to religious education.

One of the crucial facts about social evolution is that at any moment one can find scattered throughout the system the elements of innovation which will become the major evolutionary developments of the next 25 to 50 years. However, we lack the mechanisms to identify these elements of the future. We lack the means for speading new practices through the system. Although it might appear that our highly developed mass media facilities would provide us with the most effective means in the world, the fact is that the major inventions in the areas of social relations and better living do not spread very well through these indirect channels of communication. In most cases a human linking agent or consultant-trainer is needed to help convert the information into the values and attitudes and skills needed for successful change. Dissemination of social innovations requires a network of human agents capable of consultative and educational leadership, similar to the network of extension agents who spread new agricultural practices.

The Identification, Mobilization, and Use of Human Resources. The development of a productive democratic system requires the rational and flexible use of human resources to fill the leadership and other roles. There must be widespread knowledge of "who is good at what" and a readiness on the part of all participants to make their contribution. For the individual in a democracy, there is a challenging confrontation between the freedom to "do your own thing" and the responsibility to try to contribute what is needed, when and where it is needed. The social system must find ways of supporting this freedom and responsibility as complementary and integrative. To do so has many implications not only for citizenship orientation but also for the education of the young—for the development of personal interests and potentialities, the actualization of abilities, and the integration of self-other orientations. The democratic system's greatest challenge and opportunity is to support the development of individuals whose personalities and value systems enable them to integrate self-actualization and membership contribution and to use the complementary resources of those with very different life-styles.

Opportunities for Continuous Education and Reeducation. Everything else can be perfect, but still the democratic system will lack quality of operation and productivity unless there is a major commitment of personpower and budget to preservice and in-service training for both the salaried and the volunteer functions. It is frequently assumed that "goodwill is enough" or that high motivation is what is needed or that the new challenge can be coped with because "we've done something like this before." But standards of excellence are the basis of success and the core of meaningful satisfaction.

In many respects it is valid to describe a democratic society as an educational or learning society, or, as John Gardner has called it, a self-renewing society. Looking at the characteristics of a democratic system which have been identified in the previous paragraphs we see much overlap with the characteristics Gardner lists for a society that has the capability of continuous renewal and reconstruction.

With the current rate of societal change it seems likely that an increasing number of individuals will have two or three different careers during their life span. To prevent serious loss of resources to society and traumatic transitions and failures by the individual, it is crucial to organize and support a continuing education process as part of our democratic system. But just as vital a part of the educational program as this preparation for the breadwinning jobs is training for the unpaid contributions of the volunteer.

As we review the educational needs of our system at the present time, we can identify several priorities. One is the vital need for leadership training on a wider scale for those who are in, or will move into, roles of leadership responsibility in the public and private sectors of the society. Another is the need for widespread "membership training" to help all participants in the system develop the values and skills of active initiative in effectively using and influencing the resources of leadership. A particularly great need is for an extensive program of "outreach involvement and training" to bring into active membership in the system the many individuals and groups who have not been given the opportunity to participate or who are now alienated from the establishment. The demonstration of realistic caring and meaningful collaboration is one of the priorities of our democracy at the present time.

Challenges the Democratic System Faces

The significant work of a democracy is both internal and external. On the one hand, it must meet the challenges of internal development and maintenance; on the other, it must effectively influence and contribute to the larger world of neighboring systems.

In the development and maintenance of the internal system, one of the tasks is to achieve sensitivity to the type and rate of change in the conditions of individual and group life, so as to guide policies and action programs for the support and improvement of the lives of all individuals in the system. Another challenge is to find ways to help all participants develop a meaningful response to the question "Who am I?" The democratic system must try to help all participants find opportunities for satisfying personal growth and development and productive political, economical, recreational, cultural, and social participation in the community.

The external challenge facing a democracy is to establish interdependence and trust with other types of social systems based on a variety of value orientations and styles of organization. The democratic system must find ways of functioning as a responsible member of the larger intergroup society and of building up its own resources to maintain reciprocity of respect and contribution in relation to the other systems. It must also work at maintaining the respect and loyalty of its own citizenry. It is crucial to maintain an active inquiry posture in the outside world and to strengthen the development of policies and plans for making contributions to the larger interdependent collectivity.

We are not talking here just about a national democratic system; the same internal and external tasks face states, local communities, and organizations living interdependently with other organizations within a community.

Personal and Interpersonal Products and Resources of Democracy

We believe that the cluster of concepts we refer to as democracy is a set of values about an ideal to be achieved. All efforts toward democracy, whether made at the individual, interpersonal, or organized group level, are still far short of the goal of a fully democratic state of affairs and a fully democratic individual. What would such a fully democratic individual be like? What kind of members does a democratic system want and need to develop? From research findings we have derived seven dimensions of personal and interpersonal orientation and behavior which we believe represent the personal growth objectives of a democratic system. It is important to review these at the present time because they will help us to think about voluntarism as a source of strength for a democracy and of growth and development opportunity for the individuals who make up the system.

Self-Motivated Involvement, Commitment, and Participation. In the democratic personality and relationship, initiative and commitment come voluntarily from within. This does not mean that individuals do not provide stimulation and external sources of motivation for each other, or that group and social norms are not an important source of ideas and expectations that give us guidance in our membership roles. But in the context of a democratic process, an external source of stimulation and influence is voluntarily listened to and accepted as a potential resource rather than as a threat or a duty.

Confidence in Self and Openness to Others. It is a paradox of the democratic orientation that one must simultaneously have self-confidence and humility. Truly democratic individuals must be able, on the one hand, to arrive at and present their own viewpoint and, on the other, to genuinely listen to the other person. The individual must never be too arrogant or too preoccupied to listen to opposing viewpoints. As White and Lippitt have stated,

> The fully self-confident person can pass easily from enthusiastic presentation of his own ideas to an appreciative open-minded listening to points of view of others. The democratic orientation requires the blending of openness to influence from others and influence from the self. Practice in this process with others and self is perhaps the most critical aspect of the education of the young in a democratic system.[3]

Openness means enduring the discomfort of listening to divergent points of view while not necessarily giving up one's own viewpoint. This democratic combination of individualism and listening to the alternatives of others requires a readiness to tolerate ambiguity and to get challenged by the search for what most closely approximates truth in a pluralistic world of varied messages, all of which usually have some element of truth to contribute.

Fact-Oriented Realism. Much of the flexibility and problem-solving orientation in a democracy derive from a data-oriented sensitivity to present and future potentialities. The motivation to strive for objective information and feedback from the problem situation is

---

[3] White and Lippitt, *op. cit.*, p. 229.

quite complementary to the orientation of openness toward all participants. There is a close affinity between the scientific spirit and the democratic spirit. The scientist's sense of humility in the face of the immensity of the facts dealt with is psychologically akin to the true democrat's sense of humility in the face of the complexity of the ideas of other group members.

As will be seen later, the basic need for information in a democratic system generates one of the most important opportunities for volunteering. Unfortunately, in many corners of our democracy today, placing a value on "find out the facts" is often labeled a "cop out" or a substitute for taking direct action. We have failed to train many of our citizens, particularly younger ones, to understand that diagnostic fact finding is a crucial part of disciplined action which maximizes the possibilities of success and of high quality results. In the area of interpersonal group relations we all can think of examples of the backlash and side effects and frustrated failures that follow from a lack of "fact-oriented realism" to where the significant action really is or ought to be.

Freedom from Status-Mindedness or Position-Mindedness. The spirit of equality as a member and peer human is another of the vital elements of a democratic value orientation. The individual or group that is preoccupied with problems of hierarchy, position, and status is developing in an antidemocratic direction. The spirit of equality does not imply that different members have the same capacities, resources, or competencies. But it does mean that problems of status do not preoccupy individual thinking and relationships. It means that individual differences in ability and competence in some areas or aspects of a situation do not spread to other nonappropriate areas, and that an individual's self-evaluation is not distorted by some particular area of expertness or inexpertness. It means that there is a flexible movement in and out of positions of leadership or acknowledged expertness as situations and tasks change. There is sensitivity to "who's good at what" now. The spirit of equality also means sensing the possibility of setting personal goals of achievement and recognition and developing the psychological freedom to look up to and acknowledge the resources of others without finding them a threat to the self.

The Basic Orientation of Fairness. The early inculcation of the value of fairness in the young ones who are growing up in a democratic social context has been noted by many observers of cultural groups. A commitment to the notion of the equality of rights and opportunities is essential to democratic relationships. When competitive self-assertion does not become a ruling theme, theñ psychological forces in a democratic culture push toward this equality. Perhaps the most significant themes of confrontation in our national community, and in the personal self-consciousness of the members of our society today, have to do with violations of fairness: unfair treatment of the young by the older generation, of the women by the men, of the nonwhite minorities by the white majority, and of consumers by producers. Some of the most important and exciting needs for volunteering are in coping with issues of unfairness. The achieving and "policing" of fairness are great internal challenges to the democratic system.

Friendliness, Emotional Warmth, and Acceptance. One of the most impressive and consistent findings of the comparative studies of democracies, autocracies, and laissez-faire societies is that there are significant differences between the democratic situation and other situations in the levels of emotional warmth or friendliness of relationships. Attitudes of friendliness and acceptance seem to be critically necessary to make a democracy workable. Reciprocal trust and friendliness are required to support openness, to prevent or dissipate status-mindedness, to make fairness feasible, and to support the objectivity needed for a rational inquiry orientation. The French philosophers of democracy emphasized the importance of this ingredient in stressing *fraternity* equally with *liberty* and *equality*. In fact, psychological warmth, acceptance, and trust are so crucial to all the other dimensions of the democratic process that today the question is often asked, "How, in view of the increasing fragmentation, depersonalization, and polarization of our society, can the necessary conditions of interpersonal connection, acceptance, and friendliness be achieved?" Our conclusion is that voluntarism (both being a volunteer and receiving attention and service from volunteers who care) provides one of the greatest potentialities for saving and strengthening our democratic system.

The Need for Volunteers, for Volunteering, and for a
Design for Voluntarism in a Democracy

In Chapter II we will be reviewing in some detail the directions of societal change that are confronting us with critical needs for volunteer personpower. Before we take up these changes, however, we would like to make a few general derivations from our discussion of democracy to the needs for voluntarism. As we see it, a democratic system needs members with a high level of commitment to voluntary participation in the affairs of the system. In a way, our first criterion of democracy, which was widespread involvement and participation in the affairs of the society, is a statement of self-initiated, self-motivated voluntarism. Many social analysts have echoed the statement of former President Herbert Hoover that "the essence of our self-government lies outside political government. Ours is a voluntary society." [4] Secretary of Housing and Urban Development George Romney has been even more explicit:

> In every community and every state across the country we need a program for voluntary action by the people, not just government action for the people—many problems can be tackled right at home, human and social problems like education, mental illness, traffic safety, urban decay, crime, delinquency, and family deterioration, through the organization of voluntary effort. Nothing can melt such human and social problems faster than the willingness of one individual to involve himself voluntarily in helping another individual overcome his problems. [5]

Analysis of a wide range of volunteer activities reveals an interesting fact. Most volunteer activity not only represents a significant contribution of energy and skill and individual resources to the functioning of democracy, but also makes a significant contribution to the volunteer's own psychological health and self-actualization. Volunteering offers many experiences necessary to democratic personality development. It is our conclusion that individual volunteers need volunteering just as much as the community needs them. This will become clear as we review briefly some of the types of volunteer activities implied in the foregoing descriptions of the dimensions of a democratic system and of a democratic personality.

[4] Quoted in Cornuelle, Richard C., and Finch, Robert. *The New Conservative Liberal Manifesto.* San Diego: Viewpoint Boo:s, 1968. p. 109.
[5] *Ibid.,* p. 115.

Outreach Efforts To Get Participation and Involvement. In all sectors of our society, and in relation to many different opportunities and activities, one of the most pressing needs is for a corps of volunteers to help reach out to involve the inactive, the uninformed, the uninvolved, and the unconnected. A volunteer network is the only feasible and effective resource for this type of effort. It is now recognized that the volunteers should come from every sector of the community in order to function as a credible outreach network. Examples of volunteer outreach efforts would include a network of teen-agers from all subcultures working to involve junior high students in drug education activities, and an interracial, interage team interviewing all types of non-involved youth and adults to identify interests and needs.

Communicating and Linking. At many points in our analysis of the functioning of the democratic system we have indicated a need for communication between the fragmented and often polarized sections of the community which have different values, orientations, expectations, and outlooks. The mass media and the written word cannot, by themselves, begin to do the job of providing channels of communication, linkage, and collaborative coordination between the many interest groups and organizations. Volunteers are needed as binding elements in the development of a functional community. For example, older citizens and young adults could be recruited and trained as mediators between students and faculty and between teen-agers and parents. In some communities influential volunteers have been able to take the initiative in convening get-togethers of the leadership of public and private agencies that had been competitive and conflicting in their programs.

Planning and Decision Making. Traditionally, most volunteers have been used to carry out programs of activity planned by professionals. But the evidence is that the fresh viewpoint of volunteers is critically needed in the long-range planning and decision-making councils of the community and its agencies. A wide variety of volunteers and paraprofessionals bring to bear on planning and decisions very different points of view from those of the professionals.

Diagnostic Fact Finding. Realistic understanding of the increasingly disparate opinions and influences in our democracy is a necessity for effective problem solving. We have seen that the diagnostic research function is one of the most undeveloped functions in the democratic nation and community. The public opinion poll experts can do only a small part. What is needed is a continuing process of diagnosis and feedback. A network of volunteers, trained and supervised by professionals is critically needed to be the observing eyes and listening ears of any pluralistic democratic community which is seeking and exploring consensus on basic values and crucial actions. The experiences of a number of communities reveal that volunteers can be trained to do a very sophisticated job of fact finding through interviewing and observation, that they welcome the necessary training and discipline, and that they find such a volunteer experience very significant for personal growth.

Discovering and Recruiting Human Resources. George Gallup, based on one of his polls, claims that 61 million American adults would like to go to work to improve their communities if they knew what to do and how. He estimates that the time these citizens could contribute as volunteers would amount to 245 million hours a week.[6] But to begin to use such resources requires trained, competent teams of volunteers and paraprofessionals working with professional leadership to identify and recruit potential workers, link them to significant activities, and support their efforts. It is hard to imagine a more exciting volunteer job than that of being a prospector for undiscovered and underused human resources.

Taking Leadership in the Appropriate Use of Professional Expertness. The limited number of highly trained professionals in most of the areas of educational and social technology requires that we develop expertness and efficiency in making the best, most flexible use of professional expertise. The leadership and initiative of key volunteers is vitally needed here. Experimental evidence indicates that when students are trained in the attitudes and skills of making effective use of teachers they make great gains in learning, and that when hospital patients are trained to use nurses and doctors more effectively they get well more quickly.

A rapid increase in the recruiting and training of paraprofessionals and volunteers is needed to carry out many of the functions formerly performed inadequately by the overextended pro-

---

[6] *Ibid.,* p. 6.

fessional. Moreover, because of their special skills and connections, volunteers are best equipped to perform many new functions.

Protecting Equality of Rights and Opportunities. Welfare, recreation, social control, health, culture, educational services, and many other functions can be carried out effectively only if there is a widespread network of concerned volunteers ready to "be their brothers' keepers," to act as protectors, supporters, consultants, and educators. In many areas of economic, political, and social injustice, such as housing, food prices, educational opportunities, job placement, and child welfare, volunteers with a deep concern, skilled intelligence, and committed initiative are the critical leverage for justice.

Preventing an Individual from Becoming a Statistic. We noted that as a democratic system becomes urbanized and industrialized the phenomena of bigness and fragmentation get in the way of some very basic requirements of a democracy. To stay involved and committed to participation one must feel that one is being reacted to and treated as a unique individual with unique needs and interests and with an influence on what goes on around them. Classroom instruction must be individualized; help and attention in a community must be personalized. As the society continues to become more complex and the needs for personal service multiply many times, there will be an increasing lag between the number of trained professionals and the magnitude of the service job to be done. The professionals will more and more have to become the recruiters, trainers, and supporters of teams of volunteers who will carry out the basic work of human relations and individualized support for the growth and development of each child and adult.

The Need for the Opportunity To Volunteer

In the preceding paragraphs we have identified some of the needs a democratic system has for the volunteer energy, time and competence of its members. In Chapter IV we will see how much every individual needs the opportunity to be of service in order to grow toward self-actualization as a democratic caring-for-others person. The days of unequal opportunity for volunteering are passing, as are the days of the condescending "lady bountiful" and the fascinated slum explorer. The trends today are toward the true voluntarism of a democracy, where giving and receiving are reciprocal, where humility arises from genuine caring and respect rather than from concern for the future of one's soul. A married couple we interviewed recently who had been serving three years in a pool of volunteers leading discussion groups on mental health films told us with conviction and excitement, "We're sure our volunteering has done more for us than we have for the groups we've met with. We keep learning things about ourselves that strengthen our marriage and help us to be better human beings." This is closer to the picture of voluntarism in a democracy, and of voluntarism in America as we see the trends developing.

II Societal Trends Affecting Voluntarism

The present frontiers of voluntarism can be discerned by understanding the present nature of our democratic society. The future frontiers of voluntarism can be foreseen by collecting the best predictions available about this society's future directions, and by making derivations about the emergence of new needs and opportunities for volunteer personpower.

In this chapter we want to pull together societal trends predicted in a number of studies about the future. We have selected the trends we believe have the most implication for change in the individual volunteer's opportunities and functions, and for change in the number and kinds of people who will be available as potential volunteers. These trends can also be viewed as having implications for the policies and programs of the organizations and institutions that use volunteers. Here our purpose is primarily to be future-oriented and to stimulate our imagination and yours to think about images of potential. We shall be returning to these images in Chapter VIII when we present an illustrative model of human resources utilization.

We have selected eight general trends of the future for brief review in the remaining sections of this chapter, and in each case we have suggested some illustrative derivations relevant to voluntarism. We hope these derivations will provide a "start-up" for additional reflections of your own about implications for planning and for action.

The Increasing Rate and Complexity of Social and Technological Change

The Trend. The analysts of the future are in general agreement that we can expect a continuing acceleration of the rate of change in the conditions of human life. Among the results of this acceleration of change will be an increase in the complexity of the social problems to be coped with and an increase in the interdependence between the various parts of the society as they attempt to solve them.

Until very recently, most of our directions for action came from largely unexamined traditions and social norms, which provided guidance based on the assumption that the core conditions of life would remain pretty much the same. Whitehead has summarized our current confrontation very clearlly:

> Our sociological theories, our political philosophy, our practical maxims of business, our political economy, and our doctrines of education are derived from unbroken traditions and practical examples from the age of Plato . . . to the end of the last century. The whole of this tradition is warped by the vicious assumption that each generation will substantially live amid the conditions governing the lives of their fathers and will transmit these conditions to mold with equal force the lives of its children. We are living in the first period of history for which this assumption is false.[1]

Much of the content of the educational curriculum is out of date almost as soon as new books are published and new teachers are trained to teach it. Industries and other large organizations are experimenting with various concepts of flexible or temporary systems, including temporary personpower teams chosen for the complementary skills, to cope with current problems and to plan for the future. There is a great emphasis on the procedures for organizational renewal and change. The increased complexity of the problems to be solved will require new patterns of teamwork between public and private sources of money and personpower, as well as many new social inventions for collaboration, coordination, and interdependence between groups, organizations, states, and nations in solving problems. Teamwork linking the elders, the middle-aged, and the young will be critical. So will the allocation of a greater proportion of budget and human resources to continuous diagnostic fact finding and systematic planning.

Implications for Voluntarism. In the face of the rate and complexity of change, there is a tendency to become dependent on the experts. They, after all, have been involved in producing all this change, so why shouldn't they be able to tell us how to cope with it and live with it? This antivoluntarism trend must be counteracted. The experts, because of the necessary specialization of their training and orientation, cannot be expected to provide the wide perspective necessary for innovative social problem solving. There will be many

[1] Whitehead, Alfred North. *Adventures of Ideas.* New York: Macmillan Co., 1933. p. 117.

needs and opportunities for volunteers to contribute their sensitivity and perspective and value judgments in creatively dealing with and planning for change.

The trend of accelerated change obviously has major implications for organizations as well as for individual volunteers. The likelihood of rapid obsolescence of structure and function becomes greater as the rate of environmental change increases. Organizations will need to be resourceful in developing mechanisms of self-renewal and in creatively using all potential human resources. One of the problems will be the tendency for preoccupation with survival and internal change to divert energy and attention from the larger environment of interdependence with other agencies and organizations, at a time when more and more interdependence of effort and coordination of activity will be required. Volunteers with broad perspectives can be a great resource for organizations coping with these requirements of external interdependence.

Inter-agency teaming of professionals to recruit, train, and supervise volunteers will need to replace the typical competitive turfdom, and funding of inter-agency service projects.

Separation and Polarization of Social, Economic, and Political Groups

The Trend. It is generally predicted that the explosion of expectations and demands for a better life will continue to generate distrust and competition, polarization and conflict between different segments of society. A continuing development of the cohesion and potency of the peer culture among the young will widen the gap between the generations. Youth's faith in the ability of the older generation to give guidance in coping with the present and the emerging future will continue to decline. Female confrontations of the male-dominated political and economic functions will intensify, as will the attack on the double standard in sexual mores. A coalition of all racial minorities is likely to confront the racial majority. The poor are developing an increasing sense of potency and outrage in their growing conflict with the affluent. The divisions between the radicals, the liberals, and the conservatives in political life are becoming more sharp. In various areas of our economy battle lines are being drawn between consumer groups and producers. Campuses are being increasingly disrupted by divisions between administrators, faculty, and students. New bases of conflict continue to emerge on the international scene. Issues of population pressure, food supply, industrialization, and territorial control will continue to create and aggravate conflict in the foreseeable future.

Faced with the uncertainties and complexities of change and the haunting images of a better life, groupings based on religion, skin color, age, etc., would seem to furnish some hope for security and for potency in achieving goals. But the solving of complex social problems, as well as the creating of conditions for personal mental health and creativity, clearly require the building of communities of interest and action and acceptance across the lines of current social cleavages and conflicts. The necessary interdependence between polarized groups in turn requires the development of new models of creative compromise which integrate the dimensions of conflict in the meeting of needs and the solving of problems.

Implications for Voluntarism. One of the critical needs and exciting opportunities will be for volunteers, along with professionals and paraprofessionals, to become skillful in taking the third party role in conflict resolution, working to develop acceptance of the difficult concept of creative compromise and demonstrating the feasibility of dealing creatively with conflict.

Another implication is that the great variety of betterment-seeking cause groups continually being formed will be rallying points for the recruitment and intensive involvement of volunteers. The proportion of volunteers giving their time and energy to social cause groups rather than to traditional voluntary agencies will probably continue to increase.

On the other hand, many of the established community institutions and agencies, such as the churches, welfare agencies, youth-serving organizations, and school systems, have great potential for initiating integrative efforts toward new communities of interest that cut across the present polarizations. Goals of community improvement, environmental improvement, educational improvement, child care improvement, and health improvement (e.g., the fight against drug abuse and alcoholism) are shared by diverse groups and can become the basis for widespread collaborative effort, attracting the energy and commitment of all sectors of the community and providing opportunities for many exciting new frontiers of volunteer effort. Hopefully, new and more representative decision-making bodies will be formed, embracing young and old, black and white, consumer and producer, volunteer and professional.

Search for Personal Meaning, Identity, Self-Renewal, and Interpersonal Connection

One of the effects of the increasing complexity and "massness" of society is the individual's increasing sense of impotence and depersonalization. One's anchorage to a small, secure, interpersonal "home base" and community of primary relations is replaced by a medley of influence attempts, demands, expectations, and invitations to divide loyalties and diffuse energies in many often competing and conflicting directions. In this context of social flux individuals are forced to rethink their answers to the question "Who am I?" Issues of self-evaluation, self-conception, vocational and citizen roles, family roles, and interpersonal relations must be faced.

The Trends. As we look into the future we can expect a great intensification of the current trends of search for meaningful philosophies of life, search for bases of security and intimacy in new patterns of interpersonal connections and new inventions for rejecting depersonalization and "doing one's own thing" as a protest and a defense against the mass society. This experimentation and search will take many forms, both personal and collective. More time and money will be invested in programs of self-improvement and sensitivity training. There will be much experimentation with new forms of collective living. Many creative attempts will be made to adapt the basic forms and practices of religion to contemporary life situations. There will be a tremendous growth in adult education programs. The protests against bureaucracy and standardization in the processing of human needs and services will take many new innovative forms.

Implications for Voluntarism. It will be quite impossible for the great increase in demand for personalization of services to be met by professional manpower resources. Much of the leadership of the expanding programs of self-study and relationship development will have to come from teams of trained, mature volunteers and paraprofessionals. Much of the tremendous expansion of personal counseling services will be supported by the development of teams of paraprofessionals and volunteers under the leadership and supervision of professionals. George Romney's concept of "one helping one," quoted in our first chapter, offers a challenge and an opportunity for voluntarism to help deal with one of the most critical of our social problems, depersonalization, and with one of the most exciting images of potential, the search for new, more satisfying answers to the questions "Who am I?" and "Who are we?"

The Changing Nature and Meaning of Work, Achievement, Leisure, and Consumption

The Trends. The General Electric "Study of the Future" notes,

There will be a growing demand that a job be meaningful. The notion that hard or unpleasant work must be tolerated because it is unavoidable will have less and less acceptance. The concept that work is a *duty* and leisure must be earned will be more and more challenged.[2]

One of the traditional core values of our society, that self-esteem or self-worth is based on high achievement, is being challenged from many quarters today. Kenneth Benne points out one of the key issues of our current transition: "Work as we have known it may well disappear in the not too distant future from the lives of many persons." But he adds,

The important part of school life still for most educators is *school work,* not school play or the acts of voluntary service undertaken by students in fulfilling their civic role inside and outside the schools. . . . We seem strangely unprepared as people, psychologically and morally, for this pervasive change that is going on around and within us. So long as self-esteem is tied up in our patterns of evaluation and action with gainful employment, the skills, the arts, and sensitivity required for tasteful and creative consumption and play, for voluntary services to self and others, for voluntary civic services and reconstruction will remain in the periphery of social life and education.[3]

In this period of transition and rapid flux a number of values, old and new, are struggling for clarification and actualization. Is work a duty or an opportunity for voluntary commitment? Is a given standard of living something which must be earned by arduous work achievements or is it a right going along with membership in the society? Is the consuming of goods and services just as important and creative an act as the producing of goods and services? Is improvement in the skills and sensitivities

---

[2] "A Study of the Future" is an unpublished study made by General Electric.

[3] Benne, Kenneth D. "Education and the Social Sciences," a chapter in the forthcoming volume, *Social Science in the School: A Search for Rationale,* edited by Irving Morrisett and W. W. Stevens, Jr., to be published by Social Science Education Consortium, University of Colorado, Boulder, Colorado.

of living harmoniously with others as important as improving the skills of productive work achievement? Are cooperative interdependence and concern for meeting the needs of others as important as competitive assertiveness in "getting ahead"? Automation and cibernation are steadily changing the nature of our technological environment, the needs of workers, and the number of working hours. At the same time the processes of value confrontation and experimentation with new patterns of living are changing the images of potentialities for living in this changing world.

Implications for Voluntarism. The steady increase in the amount of discretionary time available to people means that there will be a vast increase in the amount of volunteer time available and in the variety of persons potentially available as volunteers. At the same time, the continuing improvement in the quality of living will mean an increase in the desire for human services of various kinds, creating many new and exciting frontiers for voluntarism.

The predictable explosion in the demand for adult education, with particular emphasis on self-improvement and cultural sensitivity courses, will create the need for large numbers of trained paraprofessionals and volunteers to help on this educational frontier. Volunteers will also be needed as guides to the various cultural and leisure time resources of the community and as leaders of recreational, educational, and religious programs.

The Postindustrial Economy

The Trend. Already today over half of the paid positions are human service jobs rather than thing-production jobs. By 1975 it is predicted that at least 75 percent of the work roles in our society will be in human service. In this postindustrial society, improvement of the quality of living and learning means finding methods to improve the delivery of human services. Research and development will focus on improving the patterns of interpersonal relationships rather than on improving the skills of working with tools and materials.

Today, teaching the generic skills of people-helping is still unheard of in most schools. As we look ahead, we can predict dramatic changes in the concepts of occupational training and in the amount of school time devoted to the applied behavioral sciences. Preparation for both paid and volunteer human service roles will begin with the first grade and continue throughout the school years. In several pioneering school systems it is already a policy for every child above the third grade to function as an educational aide to a younger child on a volunteer basis every week.

Looking into the future, we also see growing emphasis on the skills and values involved in being an intelligent, sophisticated, sensitive consumer of services. One of the interesting images of the future which we find in several organizations and communities today is the development of "human resources banks," which are really directories of "who is good at what" and "who is ready to be used by others." A very effective social studies unit for third grade children on "How To Learn from Grown-Ups" is another example of concern for improving the consumption of services. With the tremendous increase in the variety of opportunities, seductive influence attempts through the mass media and other promotion efforts, and the multiplicity of groups inviting membership, it is critical that the major focus of education be on helping the young, and their elders, become critically selective and personally integrative in their choice of activities, relationships, and involvements.

Organizations and institutions are also changing the way they are organized to produce their products, and to deliver services to consumers. There are movements towards decentralization of decision-making, production and distribution; toward "flattened out" organization charts instead of the traditional hierarchy pyramids.

Implications for Voluntarism. We foresee the development of "delivery of service teams" made up of volunteers, paraprofessionals, and professionals. Because the economy will not support a very large increase in the ratio of professionals to clients, there will be a large demand in education, medicine, and other fields for recruitment and training of volunteers as aides and co-workers.

Hopefully, another implication is that every individual from early childhood on will have opportunities and training to volunteer for significant people-hiring efforts, so that they will develop the values, the motivations, and the skills to be an effective volunteer and will view volunteer activities as vitally important opportunities for self-growth and for making their contribution to the community.

The business and political sectors of community are beginning to respond to consumer and citizen expectations and demands for higher quality of products and services by reaching out for more linkage with the community. A major means for such effort is through volunteers who are "in touch" with the needs and attitudes of the community.

Changes in the Institutions and Programs for the Socialization of the Young

The Trends. One of the most rapidly emerging social trends, and one that is of great concern to many adults, is the tendency for youth to take over the direction of their own education and socialization processes. A number of studies suggest that the movement toward self-socialization on the part of the young is not so much a rejection of their elders as it is an expression of disappointment with the lack of relevant guidance they have been receiving. Supporting this interpretation is the enthusiasm with which the young respond to invitations to go into partnership with their elders in dealing responsibly with community and national problems such as political elections, environmental deterioration, and civil rights. They eagerly seize opportunities for useful apprenticeships in social agencies and in the work world, opportunities to become involved in meaningful religious experiences, and opportunities to contribute their own artistic products—music, art, dance, and others—to the total richness of our cultural life.

Of course, there are also serious forces of destruction, alienation, and irresponsibility in youth's self-socialization process which sometimes manifest themselves in the fierce autonomy of "doing our own thing" and in the aggressive acts of rebellious violence. These would seem to predict an accelerating trend of polarization, separation, and conflict between the generations and a decline in influence by adult socialization agents and agencies, were it not for other trends which suggest the emergence of a different pattern or at least a parallel pattern. We see older peers becoming linkers and mediators between elders and the young. We see an increasing number of sensitive and sophisticated adults identified with the youth culture winning acceptance and providing linkage and resources in the development of meaningful dialogue and reciprocality of influence with the established power systems. We see senior citizens teaming up with the young in rational and creative strategies for influencing the establishment. We see the leadership of the peer culture beginning to use the consultation of professionals to develop the resources and skills needed for effective transition into core participation and influence in the larger society. Clearly much of the future creativity and stability of our society depends on the directions in which this socialization process will move. The youth are tremendously in need of the problem-solving technology and long-range strategic thinking of the applied social science professionals. At the same time they are disillusioned and distrustful about the availability of noncoercive help from the older generation.

The trends in the socialization of the young child are another area of great interest. People are getting married at an earlier age, and the attitudes toward marriage are changing rapidly. There is experimentation with various patterns of collective living in which children have an environment of a variety of parental figures rather than just two. Women are meeting with some success in their demands that the community develop child care services to permit mothers to compete and collaborate equally with fathers in employment and in community service activities. As a result of these trends, more children are experiencing a greater variety of nonparental adult socialization agents at an earlier age.

Implications for Voluntarism. The traditional youth-serving organizations will be required to reorient their policies, their programs, and their structures to meet young people's demands for relevance and shared power in decision making and program planning. The days of traditional programs of youth work and youth service are clearly numbered. Obsolescence is rapid now and will accelerate.

It seems safe to predict that there will be a great and growing need for sensitive adults—old, middle-aged, and young—to discover significant roles as volunteers in linking the younger generation to meaningful opportunities for collaboration and involvement in the larger community. As the young experiment with such complex areas as drug use, premarital and nonmarital sex relations, political activism, and alternatives to the current economic system, they have great need for the perspectives, confrontations, and emotional support of nonauthoritarian helping adults or older young people.

It will certainly be impossible for professional manpower to cope with the greatly increased demand for child care and parent substitute services. Volunteers will be needed here. The parent education and marriage education fields will also offer many opportunities for trained volunteers.

Our Natural Environment and Human Resources

The Trends. As we look ahead we can see a rising tide of sensitivity to the exploitation, pollution, neglect, and scarring of our natural environment, and to the creation of ugly and dysfunctional man-made environments—cities, mass-constructed suburbs, commercial forests of signs, and deafening waves of discordant noise. Rational approaches to problem solving will be at a premium for a while. There will be many Pied Pipers of cultish solutions, and many demands for followership. And there will be many defensive maneuvers to avoid the energy and expense of large-scale air and water clean-up, beautification, population dispersion, architectural relevance, and local and regional planning. It seems safe to predict more widespread citizen involvement than ever before in political and economic problems that have relevance for everyone. Because these problems will loom so large in the future, they will present a great potential for constructive dialogue and collaboration between the generations.

Our misuse and lack of use of our human resources is just as tragic a scandal as our misuse and overuse of our natural ones. Our indices of gross national product and of level of employment are misleading, because they hide the true facts about the tragically low level of motivated energy being contributed by our total potential humanpower pool, as well as the great misappropriations of time and energy. We can look ahead to many explosions of discontent and efforts to deal with our misuses of human resources. Women are beginning to protest once again the stereotyping that limits their roles and contributions. The blacks and other neglected minorities are being heard on their exclusion from opportunities to develop and use their talents appropriately. Large numbers of the young are expressing their discontent by withdrawing from achievement-oriented activities and from the development of the knowledge and skills required for full contribution.

Although the rate of obsolescence of particular job roles is increasing, we have made relatively little progress in providing opportunities for reorientation and retraining for new careers. Poor use of the information we have from social psychology about how to make working conditions interesting means that great masses of our workers work at a very low level of motivation, spend a great deal of energy on peer collusions to restrict their output, and get their satisfactions from success in conflicts with management rather than from pride in work. The exploitation and pollution of our natural environment are indeed serious, but the underdevelopment and dissipation of our human resources are just as dangerous for the vitality and future of our society.

Implications for Voluntarism. The political action projects, both local and national, required to cope with the issue of quality of environment must depend primarily on volunteer energies. To avoid blind alleys and false starts the volunteers will of course need to use effectively the most expert help available, but volunteer effort will be the real basis for any success in winning and guaranteeing a future for ourselves in a livable habitat.

As we have indicated earlier, the organization and use of human resource banks can be a tremendously important and exciting effort for volunteers. One of the greatest needs here is to find ways to induce more and more fellow citizens to get out of their passive rut and to give their time and energy to activities that promote personal growth and improve the community. Enticing others to explore and develop their human potential is indeed an exciting challenge for volunteers and their professional helpers.

Involvement in a World Society [4]

The Trend. Related to the first trend we identified, that of the increasing rate and complexity of change and the necessary increase in the interdependence of those segments of the society involved in coping with the change, is the trend toward international collaboration in problem solving. Many of our current

---

[4] Much of our discussion here has been derived from Kenneth Benne, *op. cit.,* p. 5.

and future problems require international or worldwide effort if there is to be any chance of successful coping: the problems of peace, population, pollution, poverty, food supply, and natural resources, among others. As Benne puts it, "Both human survival and effective meeting of human needs require effective actions on a world scale along with the development of adequate instrumentalities to form, inform, and sanction such actions." But, Benne continues,

> Efforts by nationals to bring world-minded attitudes and criteria to bear in criticism and improvement of national policies, whether in public forms or in educational programs, are condemned or suspended as traitorous or disloyal by large segments of the totally committed or deeply anxious segments of the national population, and not infrequently by the national governments.

In our current phase of national and world development, "nationalism" is still linked in the minds of vast numbers of people with liberation and freedom and redefinition of personal identity. Citizenship has been defined in national terms, and no effective alternative citizenship concept has been developed. The rationality of those in many nations who now advocate a transfer of allegiance from national symbols and authorities to transnational ones is, as Benne says,

> ... forced into conflict with their loyalty when questions of "national good" and "world good" come to the fore in choice and in action. The energy and thought tends to dissipate itself in rationalization of national loyalties and into subversions of these loyalties rather than to inventing ways of reconciling world and national interest and of advancing both.

One of the great challenges of the future will be to invent and test out new ways of accepting and dealing creatively with confronting multiple loyalties within the self. We have referred to this previously as discovering the potential of creative compromise. One of the barriers to personal and collective growth toward effective membership in a pluralistic world is the negative connotations we have ascribed to the idea of compromise. Here indeed is a major challenge for reeducating ourselves and educating the next generation.

Implications for Voluntarism. A good starting point in preparing for the future would be to set up opportunities for ourselves and for the younger generation to join in significant probing dialogues with persons of different national cultures. The initiation and leadership of such activities could be a very challenging function for volunteers. Initiating exchanges of information and points of view with groups in other countries has proved to be a very feasible and meaningful pattern, as yet undeveloped in most schools, recreational and political systems, and communities.

Many of our national volunteer organizations have international counterparts and connections. Most of them have developed some programs of international exchange. These could be the focus and the leverage for interagency collaboration in the development of large enough programs of international dialogue to begin to have political and economic significance. The opportunities for volunteer leadership seem very substantial. The freedom of the policy-making volunteers from immediate operating demands would facilitate openness to change.

Conclusion

We hope this discussion of societal trends with implications for the development of voluntarism has been a springboard for your own thinking about the future. In the next chapter, we want to turn our attention to the many trends emerging *within* the world of voluntarism which will also have a significant impact in the years ahead.

III Emerging Changes in the World of Voluntarism

The trends and changes emerging in the world of voluntarism are exciting because they indicate that voluntarism is becoming one of the major means of providing human services. That is, agencies and institutions, both private and public, are extending their activities, programs, and services through a greatly increased use of volunteer personpower. As the number of hours, days, and years of paid work decline, more and more people will be involved in meaningful volunteer activity. Indeed the Administration has made it clear that voluntarism is one of the ways in which the citizens of this country can increase their help to each other and to themselves, and thus make the democratic system work more effectively. As we look at emerging changes and the current and future need for volunteer personpower, we can make several assumptions.

Some Background Generalizations

The needs for human service in today's complex, interdependent, and changing society go far beyond the economic potential for paid services. For example, the support for the public school and for other public and private agency programs is not likely to provide a base for any changes in the ratio of professionals to clients. The teacher-to-student ratio will tend to remain about 1 to 25 or 30. At the same time, there is need for more personal and individualized services. The clear implication is for the development of teams of volunteers and paraprofessionals working with professionals to extend services.

The role of the professional in many human situations is becoming that of manager. He/She is in-service trainer or consultant to team members, leader of planning and evaluation, and coordinator of the teamwork of those working together. This is a new role for the professional person. Instead of giving direct service to clients, the professional gives direct service to members of the team.

The outreach, involvement, and caring efforts needed in working with the neglected, the rejected, and the powerless require a mobilization of the efforts of a widespread network of local volunteers—people who live in the same area as the clients and who become skillful in helping their peers. Local volunteers avoid the communication gaps and distrust that often arise between professionals and clients of different racial, ethnic, economic, and educational backgrounds.

There is a serious lack of preparation for competent and motivated voluntarism in the early learning experiences of children, particularly of those in underdeveloped neighborhoods. Most of the training for voluntarism and the development of attitudes and values concerning volunteering should occur during the early years of school. The curriculum and the educational experience program should emphasize the giving and receiving of help. Many schools are offering very exciting opportunities for peers to help each other and for older students to work with younger students. Such opportunities need to be a part of the upper elementary and early secondary school years, followed by opportunities for in-school and out-of-school apprenticeship.

The school, through tutorial and cross-age projects, can provide many opportunities for career explorations, in addition to training for the volunteer role. During these explorations of occupational roles, the students need to have a continuing "practicum seminar" providing opportunities for them to relate their field experience to their classwork and to share and analyze personal experiences, value problems, inquiries about the world of work, analyses of occupational trends, and connections between the requirements of various types of occupational roles and academic training.

One of the needs of citizens in a democratic society is to be able to help voluntarily in the problem-solving processes of the society. Yet, in almost any newspaper, one can find illustrations of avoidance by neighbors or fellow citizens when collective action is needed to solve a problem. Much experience and skill can be gained through training and volunteer work involved with social problem solving. For example, when students have received training in skills revelant to solving campus problems and have then had some successful experiences with collective and collaborative action, they are much more able to make decisions, solve problems, and help others do so. They are also more willing to take risks. An example of such training is a volunteer curriculum where teams of four students each identify a problematic aspect of their environment with which they would like to try to work. In their laboratory course they study the methods of action research and problem solving and carry through a diagnosis of their problem situation, developing a strategy for problem solving with consultation from the teacher and others, including their peers. They then carry through a voluntary action effort and an evaluation of its success.

In a world in which a small percentage of the population will be able to provide all of the goods and services for the rest, it will be extremely necessary to provide avenues of meaningful volunteer activity for people who are not fully employed. It will be increasingly important that agencies and institutions offer worthwhile opportunities for volunteer participation.

Members of the various generations do not now communicate well with each other. To improve their dialogue possibilities and bridge some of the communication gaps between them, they will need opportunities to work together in intergenerational volunteer teams. Examples of this kind of activity include tutorial projects with olders and youngers working as teams to tutor older people who need to learn the English language, and intergenerational teams visiting lonely patients in nursing homes.

Policy making and action taking in a democracy assume and require widespread involvement and are totally dependent on commitment of volunteer time and energy. As the society becomes larger, more differentiated, and more diffuse, as its functions of maintenance and growth become more complex, more volunteer time and energy must be given to citizenship activities if the society is to continue to evolve as a democratic one. As the rate of social change increases, and as change becomes a more complex process, there is increased need for the perspective and energy of volunteers to create the necessary confrontations to the establishment manned by professionals and technicians.

Traditionally, volunteers have been recruited only from the upper and upper-middle class white Protestant sectors of the community. There has been and still is unequal opportunity to volunteer. Because of the chances for personal growth and social recognition provided by volunteering, as well as the great need for volunteers with special sensitivity to the alienated and neglected members of the community, there must be an active effort to spread the opportunities for voluntarism throughout the community.

Trends Toward Greater Volunteer Utilization

As our society has been changing, so have the values and practices regarding the use of volunteers. Also, as we move from an industrial to a post industrial society, more human services are needed, demanded, and being made available. Costs and available funds cannot keep pace with demands, and more volunteers will continue to be needed to help professionals provide these services. Some of the recent trends in the world of voluntarism may help us look ahead to fuller community utilization of volunteers.

1. One obvious trend is that *the importance of volunteering and voluntarism is being discussed more widely* at all levels of the society and the community. The federal administration, many state and local governments, and industries are promoting and supporting the use of volunteers. For example, some legislation now provides that public social welfare departments must have volunteers on their advisory committees. Sometimes there is a requirement that a civil servant be hired or promoted to be a paid professional director of the volunteer program.

2. Another trend is for both private and public employers to put *more emphasis on the value of volunteer service on the part of their employees.* While it is not entirely new for private businesses to encourage their executives and subexecutives to participate in community affairs and to have their families participate, it is now increasingly felt that workers from all levels should become active volunteers in the community. Some telephone companies now encourage employees through small group training to participate in political, social, and educational activities in their communities.

3. A great effort is currently being made to recruit *new volunteer man, woman, and child power* including people who have never volunteered before, from all economic, life style, racial, religious, and nationality backgrounds. The volunteer opportunities include a variety of decision-making, catalyst, change agent, cause oriented, service activities. There is a strong trend to involve educational, recreational, and health students in the social services of the community. Greater efforts are being made to recruit retired volunteers, and there is an increasing trend to use technical and professional resources on an extracurricular basis. Professionals are being

recruited to give their volunteer time to tutorial projects, urban action commissions, fair housing committees, and other causes. There are also increasing numbers of young volunteers anxious to serve, often more than the agencies can place.

4. In another trend, volunteers are serving as *links between the institution and its clients.* Examples are the doctor's aide who is a link between the doctor and the patient; the volunteer who serves as a community aide and tries to link parents to the school and vice versa; the public health center aide who informs community residents of available services for which they are eligible.

5. Among the new patterns of volunteer participation is *the use of pairs.* For example, a middle class volunteer is paired with a local poverty area volunteer to lead a new youth group in a poverty area.

6. Another new pattern is *the use of teams of professionals, paraprofessionals, and volunteers* to work together in classroom teaching, medical service, child care activities, social work services, tutoring, and many other areas of community activity. New ways are being found to divide service to clients by analyzing the different resources of the professional, the paraprofessional, and the volunteer. In other words, there is some search to see who can do what piece of the job best.

7. The concept is emerging that *volunteers are an important and integral part of the service team.* Many agencies and organizations are finding that fewer volunteers want desk and clerical jobs. They prefer social action and direct service to clients. There is a growing emphasis on this new volunteer role.

8. Another development is *the career ladder of voluntarism,* which encourages moving up or over from one job level to another. In some cases this means using volunteer experiences as training for, and stepping stones to, paid career jobs in such fields as education, recreation, health, probation, and parole. In other cases it means that types of work formerly labeled professional are now being entrusted to skilled volunteers. For instance, a family service agency is recruiting volunteers and training them to be assistants or aides to the social worker. They are learning how to make home visits and how to counsel selected clients.

9. Not only new levels of work, but also *many new settings are now open* to volunteers. Volunteers are sought for various roles in the field of corrections, long closed to them. Public schools are achieving significant extension of their services by allowing volunteers to work directly with children in educational activities. City and state governments are beginning to recruit volunteers for important

functions in relation to planning and urban renewal. The development of the "Hot Line" movement with over-the-phone counseling by trained volunteers is another new kind of volunteer opportunity. The counselors must deal with a variety of problems such as mental illness and threatened suicide.

10. Another trend we have found in many areas is that *the clients of agencies are becoming volunteers themselves.* In one project where volunteers were educating people to participate in local elections, many of the learners in turn became volunteer teachers of others, because of their enthusiasm for the project. Another example is the welfare client who now sits on welfare department advisory committees.

11. As volunteers representing a broader cross section of the community are being used in new patterns and new settings, agencies are beginning to realize that they *need to include budget items for enabling funds for volunteers,* such as transportation, parking, conference registration, baby sitting, and meals. Both local and national organizations are now picking up these tabs for their volunteers.

12. We have noticed another interesting trend in our observations of the world of voluntarism: there is *more use of volunteers on a temporary or ad hoc basis.* Volunteers may be recruited to do short-term tutoring, to act as temporary advisers, to work on a crash project, or sit on a temporary committee or task force, without necessarily being recruited to serve forever.

13. There is a *new emphasis on the importance of training for the volunteer.* New opportunities for volunteer training are being offered by university extensions, by adult education departments, and by agencies acting collaboratively for this purpose. These opportunities include courses and seminars for the new volunteer, the board member, and the direct service volunteer. Increasingly, the volunteer is being sought to help plan the training so that it will meet the needs. Often the training is given at various points in the volunteer's career, rather than all at the beginning, so that it becomes of ongoing and maximum usefulness. A corollary trend is toward more training of volunteer trainers; that is, more volunteers are being trained to train other volunteers. In community action programs local people have been trained in particular community skills and then trained to help other people learn to participate. Also, more audiovisual training materials are available and being developed. They deal with such topics as racism, better human relations in the school, and developing the volunteer community. There is likewise an increase in the use of behavioral scientists as consultants to help in the training of volunteers and volunteer trainers.

Some of the professional schools are becoming concerned about the need for better training of professionals to work with volunteers. These include schools of social work, education, medicine, recreation, and public health. It is necessary for professionals in all the "people-helping" fields to have skills in the recruitment, orientation, training, retraining, supervision, and development of volunteers and volunteer programs.

14. Another very significant development in voluntarism is the *emergence of autonomous volunteer movements* to supplement the traditional agencies and institutions. Various types of action and process groups have mobilized volunteer efforts—for example, those formed to protect consumers from unfair practices in relation to rent, food, prices, legal services, and credit. Some groups have developed "watchdog" programs manned by volunteers. Others are providing consultation and educational services to consumers to help them better use the human and material resources available in the medical, social, legal, health, welfare, and recreational fields. Often these voluntary cause groups are grass roots organizations whose members really know and understand the need for their services. The following are some of the characteristics of these groups:

- They often don't have formal, written by-laws.
- There is usually a conscious effort on the part of the leadership to build a participatory democracy.
- They are energized around specific social issues.
- They often have a high mortality rate or short life span, often because their causes are temporary ones.
- They are able to take risks that many of the establishment organizations cannot take, because the viability of these voluntary cause organizations depends on continuously meeting needs of members, rather than organizational needs per se.
- By and large, they are poorly funded and understaffed.
- They are highly suspicious of establishment help and demand that "outsiders" take an advocacy role.
- They operate informally and devise only such ground rules as seem necessary.
- They seem to find it hard to collaborate with other groups which have similar goals but come from other racial, regional, and economic levels.[1]

15. Also there is a *greater emphasis on quality control of services*. With increasing concern about shrinking dollar resources,

[1] These characteristics were identified by Harold Kellner in "Grass Roots Voluntarism," a proposal for an action-research program in the Boston metropolitan area.

more effective record keeping and accountability are being stressed. Funding bodies want to know both the cost of volunteer programs as well as the benefits of volunteer programs as well as the benefits of volunteer services translated into dollar value.

16. *New roles for volunteers are emerging.* These include volunteers being trained to do research, evaluation and documentation. Also, some volunteers are utilizing their time as advocates in such areas as child and family advocacy, anti-rape centers, and legal aid for the poor.

A different role is that of the volunteer methodological advocate. This is a person who acts as a mediator between two confronting, different points of view, trying to help both parties find a creative solution or compromise. More volunteers are acting as administrative volunteers, thus extending the services of an administrative system. Indeed in these and other new roles, the volunteer *extends* the professional services available. It is the purof the volunteer to extend, to humanize, to individualize human service, *not to replace paid workers.*

17. It is evident that *motivations to volunteer are changing* from the old emphasis on "doing your citizenship duty" or pure altruism. Today the motivations to volunteer may include: preparation for and/or exploration of paid employment; causing change to happen; people with similar problems counseling each other (e.g. breast cancer patients, drug users, etc.); wanting to be where the action is; deep concern about causes such as ecology, the women's movement, minority rights, etc.; self development and growth; wish to be with like minded people; staying in the mainstream (this is particularly true for the older volunteer).

18. *New opportunities for paid professionals in the volunteer world.* As more volunteers have opportunity to serve in the people helping fields, more professionals are being hired to administer and supervise these programs. The professional opportunities are as administrators or directors, supervisors, trainers and consultants to volunteers and volunteer programs in all sectors of the community (see Chapter VIII page 98).

19. There is an emergence of *fringe benefits for volunteers.* Many volunteers are now covered by Workmen's Compensation and other insurance policies. Also, records are kept on what volunteers do, their evaluations, and whom they work with. These facts can then be used to draw up resumes that help volunteers, who so desire, to get paid jobs.

Training opportunities for volunteers are being made increasingly available within and outside of the organization. Sometimes some of the costs of this training are defrayed by the host agency. Though volunteers do not get paid money for their services, they do receive other benefits and satisfactions from their services.

Confrontations and Resistances to the Use of Volunteers

Professional-Volunteer Relationship Tensions

Running parallel to the trends toward a fuller mobilization of volunteer power are trends of resistance and confrontation to the active and widespread use of volunteers. The efforts to use volunteers in new areas and to promote them to new levels of responsibility are met in some quarters with cautiousness, resistance, and rejection. One type of resistance arises from the increasing pressures of professional and technical training certification. In the pursuit of a higher quality of professionalism, protective associations seek to maintain standards and to clarify the boundaries of professional competence. Traditionally, there has been a very distinct and complete separation between the professional and volunteers.

1. The *increase in ambiguity about competence* increases the professional's resistance to extending fuller participation to volunteers as members of the service team and allowing them to do more meaningful and more "professional" tasks. The specific and highly individual resources of both the volunteer and the professional are not used to their fullest in situations where such resistance is a factor.

2. The current trend for the professional to become more of a trainer and consultant to teams of volunteers and paraprofessionals results in *much less contact between the professional and the client.* The professional loses the immediate interpersonal reward that flows from the response of clients. In many cases they feel threatened by the volunteers' moving into the most meaningful direct contact with clients—for example, when volunteer case aides deal directly with the client while the professional social worker deals only with the case aide.

3. Often, as the need for volunteer training expands, the professional becomes more and more aware of the *lack of*

background and ability to be a trainer. The feelings of incompetence in this area lead to resistance of further programs of volunteer mobilization.

4. Changes in the professional curricula are slower than changes in the outside world. In many cases, therefore, the *local volunteers have more relevant information and skills than the professionals.* This situation is, of course, threatening to the professionals and often leads them to resist maximum utilization of the volunteers.

5. Particularly in metropolitan areas, today's *volunteers are often recruited from the same area as the clients* of the human service organizations. Consequently, they may have a much closer association with the clients, more sensitivity to their situation, and greater ease in getting accepted than the professionals have. This state of affairs, which the professionals naturally perceive as a threat, makes it hard for them to give the necessary help and support to the volunteers. It is particularly apt to arise where the middle class white professional is working with clients and volunteers of a different race, age, social and economic background.

6. Many volunteers are proving difficult for the professionals because they may be *very articulate about their expectations* and their status, and critical of their assignments if they don't like them or don't understand them. Many volunteers are finding in some of the newer, more autonomous cause programs greater excitement, more freedom from restraint, and wider opportunities for meaningful participation than in the traditional volunteer roles and agencies.

7. Further hampering the appropriate use of volunteers are the *lack of interagency sharing* of program priorities and client populations and the lack of collaboration in the identifying, recruiting and training of volunteers. Thus a highly competitive orientation develops, and a possessive attitude about "our clients" and "our volunteers."

8. One of the bases of tension between volunteers and professionals is *the tradition of "confidentiality"* which has excluded volunteers from the inner workings and records of many agencies. As volunteers assume more responsibility this tradition becomes dysfunctional, but professionals still tend to use it as a basis for resistance to full volunteer participation.

9. A number of *myths maintained by professionals* contribute to their resistance to volunteers: "They don't get paid, so they can

come and go as they please"; "They hire us, so they think they are
better than we are and can fire us"; "They are volunteers and
therefore not professionally competent"; "They only spend a few
hours a week, and they are not as committed as the professional";
"They meet their needs and not ours, and they take too much
professional time to consult with and to supervise"; "They crowd
an already crowded facility"—these are some of the myths.

As we look at these causes of professional resistance in light of
the changes toward more widespread use of volunteers in more
significant roles, we can predict that a great deal of tension will
continue to develop. Many professionals will continue to resist
using volunteers and paraprofessionals fully. Obviously we need to
work with professionals in the professional schools and on the job
to help them develop more favorable attitudes toward the use of
the vast resources of volunteer personpower.

Confrontations from the Women's Movement and the Unions

Resistance and confrontations are coming from two additional
sources. The Women's Movement has clearly and forcefully
declared its opposition to women doing "second class citizen"
work without pay. Some of the objections have been aimed mainly
at menial direct service volunteer jobs, at lack of contracts between volunteers and the organizations where they serve, and at
lack of insurance coverage for volunteers.

These confrontations have been most valuable in many ways,
because they have forced persons and organizations utilizing
volunteer human resources to take a critical look at what they are
doing, and to make a number of changes in their practices and
policies.

Some Unions are objecting to volunteers working in more new
spaces and places. They worry because they feel volunteers have
displaced or will replace paid workers. Especially in times of
strained budgets, this objection is easy to appreciate and understand. However, as stated earlier in this book, volunteers are
recruited to help professionals help clients. Volunteers add a different dimension to the team serving clients. Usually they are
available for restricted time periods only. It is important that all
systems utilizing volunteers have clear policies and practices
about the role and function of the volunteer as a volunteer. It is
not the purpose of the volunteer movement in the United States to

take paid work away from anyone. It must also be taken into account, that there is a large discrepancy between the increasing need and demand for humane human services, and the budgets and people available to supply these needs.

IV The Motivational Dynamics of Voluntarism

In the previous chapters we have seen how important it is to the present and future creative functioning and development of democratic systems to increase the amount, the quality, and the variety of volunteer service. In this chapter we want to focus on the motivation of volunteers. Successful voluntarism will come about only if individuals feel motivated toward it. "Improvement in the delivery of services" remains an abstract phrase unless more and more individuals become motivated to volunteer their time and energy, to make the commitment, and to achieve the skills needed to help provide these services.

Understanding and supporting the motivation of the individual volunteer are critical. The forces that influence and determine the decision to volunteer one's time and energy are located both inside and outside the individual decider. Common motivating forces include the feelings of "I want to because it sounds fun and interesting," "It's my duty to help," "Something needs to be done," "They want and need me," "Unless I join in and help they can't be successful," "This organization has to become more relevant, and I want to help it change now", and "I want to explore this field to see if I'd like to work for pay there." Each of these is a quite separate and distinct force.

Of course, before the decision to volunteer can be faced at all, the opportunity to volunteer must be made available to the individual. Administrators and other professionals have to define activities as needing volunteer help and have to decide to recruit volunteers. The forces that determine these decisions of the professionals and policy makers are again both internal and external. Again, they vary widely, from the feeling of "I need their help" to "Policy and budget require me to work with volunteers" to "They need me and I need them" to "They are a necessary evil, more bother than help" to "It costs money to administer a good volunteer program."

In this chapter we want to look at motivational dynamics both within the life space of the volunteer and within the life space and organizational space of the professional who uses volunteers. We hope the following questions will help us in our exploration of the motivation of the volunteer:

1. What are the key forces involved in the individual decision to volunteer or to avoid volunteering? To put a significant proportion of one's discretionary time and energy into volunteer activity or to make only a minor contribution?

2. What forces guide the decision as to the type of volunteer activity one will commit oneself to?

3. What are the bases of the decision to make a commitment to personal learning, to develop the skills needed to make a high quality contribution in one's volunteer work?

4. What are the bases of the decision to continue or discontinue volunteer work after a period of service?

In exploring the life space of the users of volunteers we need to try to understand their motivational bases—

1. The decision to perceive and accept the need for volunteers.

2. The decisions to define and provide particular volunteer jobs and to recruit particular volunteers for these roles.

3. The decision to give priority to the support, training and growth of volunteers.

4. The comitment to learn from and to be influenced by interaction and collaboration with volunteers.

To Volunteer or Not To Volunteer

Let's assume for a moment that we are listening in to the thoughts of individuals trying to decide whether to commit their volunteer time and energy to some activity or program. We find we can organize what they are thinking in several ways. First of all, we can break down the forces motivating them into two main groups: those pushing toward a "yes" and those pushing toward a "no" decision on volunteering. These two sets of forces are listed in the decision force field in figure 1, which follows the model of Kurt Lewin.[1] Each set is further subdivided into motivational forces that come from inside the self (what Lewin has called "Own Forces"), those that originate outside the self, in the relationship one has with other persons and the membership one has in certain groups ("Interpersonal and Group Member Forces"), and those based on characteristics of

[1] Lewin, Kurt. "Frontiers in Group Dynamics: Concept, Method, and Reality in Social Science; Social Equilibria and Social Change." *Human Relations* 1:5-41; June 1947.

the total situation of the decision maker: issues of geography, time and space, transportation, economics, etc. ("Situational Forces").

All the forces shown in figure 1 are not operating in any one person facing any one decision, of course. The list is a summary across a number of persons and decisions. Moreover, these forces are not equally strong, and they do not have the same strength for different persons. If we were representing a particular person making a particular decision, only some of the forces would be relevant, and their strength would be quite variable. As you study figure 1, you can no doubt make additions to it from your own experience and from that of volunteers you have known.

Figure 1.   The Decision To Volunteer or Not To Volunteer

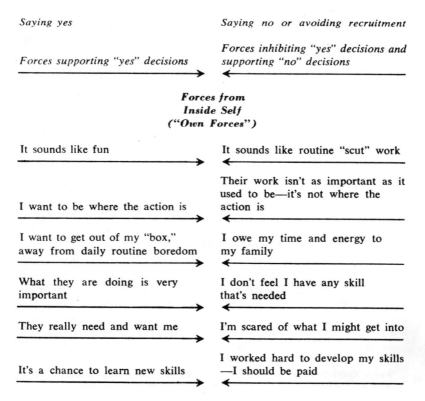

Saying yes   *Saying no or avoiding recruitment*

Forces supporting "yes" decisions   *Forces inhibiting "yes" decisions and supporting "no" decisions*

**Forces from
Inside Self
("Own Forces")**

It sounds like fun   It sounds like routine "scut" work

I want to be where the action is   Their work isn't as important as it used to be—it's not where the action is

I want to get out of my "box," away from daily routine boredom   I owe my time and energy to my family

What they are doing is very important   I don't feel I have any skill that's needed

They really need and want me   I'm scared of what I might get into

It's a chance to learn new skills   I worked hard to develop my skills —I should be paid

It's a chance to learn things that
would help me get ahead

→

I think I am too old for that

←

The visibility could help me on
my job

→

It's not clear what kind of help
and support I'd get

←

It could help me with my
personal life

→

The last time I said yes it was
a waste of my time

←

It might tie me down at times—
I'd want to be free to do
other things

←

I've gotten a lot of help. Now
it's my turn to repay

→

It's a critical need; I've got to
do my part

→

I need to earn extra money in
my spare time

←

I need something to do

→

It's unpopular; I'll be involved
in conflict

←

I'll have a chance to really
influence what happens

→

I'll waste my time if I don't
commit it to something

→

Forces from Relations with Others ("Interpersonal and Group Member Forces")

Service is a tradition in our
family—it's expected

→

They don't trust volunteers to
do the important things

←

It's one of the things our group
members do, part of our program

→

My colleagues would raise their
eyebrows at my getting into that

←

My best friend is asking me

→

I might lose my job

←

He's an important person. I don't
feel I can say no

→

My family would object

←

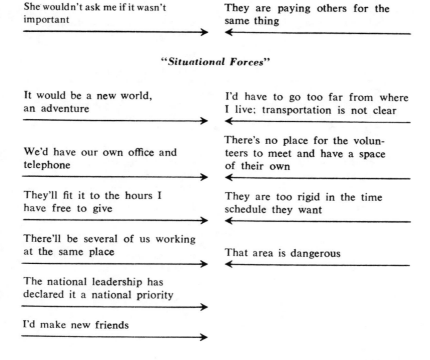

She wouldn't ask me if it wasn't
important
                                        They are paying others for the
                                        same thing

"*Situational Forces*"

It would be a new world,
an adventure
                                        I'd have to go too far from where
                                        I live; transportation is not clear

                                        There's no place for the volun-
We'd have our own office and   teers to meet and have a space
telephone   of their own

They'll fit it to the hours I   They are too rigid in the time
have free to give   schedule they want

There'll be several of us working
at the same place   That area is dangerous

The national leadership has
declared it a national priority

I'd make new friends

In observing the force field we notice that some volunteers seem to put major motivational emphasis on the *self-actualization possibilities* of an opportunity to volunteer, while others put a contrasting emphasis on *service, duty, and the repayment of a "service received" debt.* The self-actualizers see opportunities for learning, for excitement, for personal growth, while the servers see opportunities for significant contributions, for the meeting of needs, and for action relevance in the society. No doubt for many volunteers both of these bases of motivation are important, but they certainly have very different priority for different types of persons and in different decision situations.

A related contrast in motivational orientations seems to be between what we might call *inner-oriented* and *other-oriented* volunteers. The inner-oriented put more weight on the "Own Forces" in the situation—their own feelings, their own sense of relevance, and their own values—as guidelines for decisions. The other-oriented decision makers are more influenced by the norms of their group, by the potential visibility and status of the volunteer activity, by its potential consequences for their job and social relationships, and by situational factors of risk and support.

A third dimension of difference in motivations we might label the dimension of *action* versus *reflection and policy*. For some volunteers the meaningful opportunity is the one that provides the excitement of direct action with clients and the opportunity to get feedback through interaction and "seeing things happen." Other volunteers feel more comfortable and get more satisfaction in a more reflective and removed type of volunteer activity, such as service on committees and policy-making boards.

Probably closely related is the contrast between potential volunteers who give priority to the opportunities for *power and influence* and those who are primarily interested in the opportunities for *emotional associations* with others. For the former group a key source of motivation is the perceived opportunity to get into a position of influence, decision making, and activity designing. The latter group looks forward to the interaction with other adults or with children, to the chance to "share" themselves and to work on a team with others.

Another important difference seems to be that some volunteers identify with *the larger community and its welfare;* they think in terms of significant community needs to be met through their service. Criteria of social significance and community relevance are important to them in choosing volunteer activities. Other volunteers are oriented primarily to the *interpersonal meanings* and *group membership meanings* of the particular volunteer opportunity. Their decisions to volunteer are determined to a high degree by the image of the people they would be working with, the type of interpersonal support they would receive, and the meaning the activity would have for their friends, their family, and the groups they belong to. Theirs is a very concrete interpersonal world rather than the more abstract social problem world.

Yet another interesting dimension of difference among potential volunteers we have defined by the three terms *autonomy-oriented, interdependence-oriented,* and *dependence- or support-oriented.* As we review the forces listed in figure 1, we see that for autonomy-oriented individuals a very important condition for volunteering is the freedom to "do one's own thing," to get away from routines and boredom, to take some risks and find some new excitement. Interdependence-oriented individuals value peer relationships and opportunities for colleagueship and mutuality of support and working relationships. For these volunteers the human relations aspect of the peer relationship on the job is a critical factor. Support-oriented individuals want a clearly defined job to do, with clear arrangements for training and on-the-job supervision and help. They want to be sure that what they are being assigned to do is something they will be competent and comfortable in doing. These volunteers place a high value on the guidelines of tradition and well-developed norms and procedures, in contrast to the autonomous volunteers, who prefer new experiences, risk, and freedom from tradition and normative expectations and demands.

As we think about different types of roles and opportunities for volunteers, we begin to sense the importance of finding ways to match the right volunteers to the right opportunities and situations, to take account of individual differences in need for support, and to shift roles and working situations to correct "poor fits."

To Continue or Drop Out

After volunteers agree to serve and have become involved in volunteer activities they are faced with the questions of whether or not they like the work, whether or not to continue, and whether or not to put more or less energy into the activity. Volunteers by their definition can change their minds more readily than professional persons. Also, volunteers make the decision as to how much time and energy to devote to volunteer activities.

Let's once again listen in on a population of decision makers, This time they will be volunteers trying to decide whether to give more or less energy and time to a particular activity, and whether to continue or discontinue their commitment. We shall use the force field in figure 2 as a guide to start us thinking in a systematic way about this area of volunteer motivation. Again we can divide into several clusters the factors that decrease commitment or lead volunteers to discontinue their volunteer work.

One group of volunteers seems to be saying that their major source of disappointment and discontent is the discrepancy be-

tween what they have found in their volunteer activity and what
they were led by their recruiters to believe it would be like.
The *unreal expectations given in recruitment* are a frequent

Figure 2. The Decision To Continue, Increase Commitment, or Drop Out

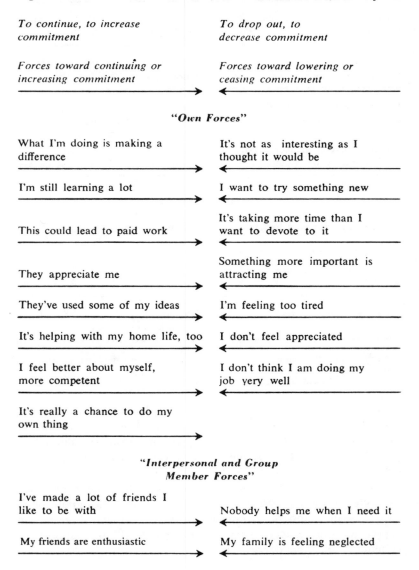

*To continue, to increase
commitment*

*To drop out, to
decrease commitment*

*Forces toward continuing or
increasing commitment*

*Forces toward lowering or
ceasing commitment*

"Own Forces"

What I'm doing is making a
difference

It's not as interesting as I
thought it would be

I'm still learning a lot

I want to try something new

This could lead to paid work

It's taking more time than I
want to devote to it

They appreciate me

Something more important is
attracting me

They've used some of my ideas

I'm feeling too tired

It's helping with my home life, too

I don't feel appreciated

I feel better about myself,
more competent

I don't think I am doing my
job very well

It's really a chance to do my
own thing

**"Interpersonal and Group
Member Forces"**

I've made a lot of friends I
like to be with

Nobody helps me when I need it

My friends are enthusiastic

My family is feeling neglected

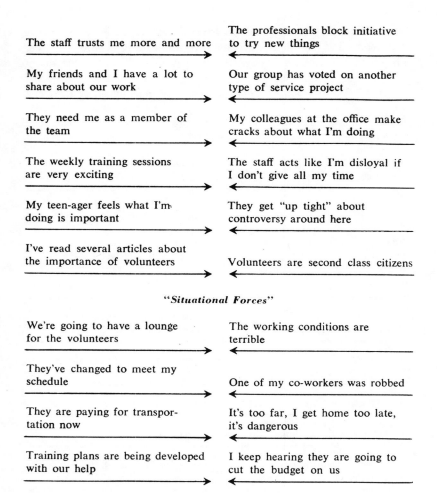

The staff trusts me more and more ⟶   ⟵ The professionals block initiative to try new things

My friends and I have a lot to share about our work ⟶   ⟵ Our group has voted on another type of service project

They need me as a member of the team ⟶   ⟵ My colleagues at the office make cracks about what I'm doing

The weekly training sessions are very exciting ⟶   ⟵ The staff acts like I'm disloyal if I don't give all my time

My teen-ager feels what I'm doing is important ⟶   ⟵ They get "up tight" about controversy around here

I've read several articles about the importance of volunteers ⟶   ⟵ Volunteers are second class citizens

"Situational Forces"

We're going to have a lounge for the volunteers ⟶   ⟵ The working conditions are terrible

They've changed to meet my schedule ⟶   ⟵ One of my co-workers was robbed

They are paying for transportation now ⟶   ⟵ It's too far, I get home too late, it's dangerous

Training plans are being developed with our help ⟶   ⟵ I keep hearing they are going to cut the budget on us

cause of "motivational shock" later on. Discrepancies between expectation and reality may be discovered in the amount of time required for the activity, the type of work, the amount of support from the professionals, the type of clients, the available facilities, and many other areas.

Another important theme is the *lack of appreciative feedback* from clients and co-workers. This may result in doubt about one's adequacy in doing the volunteer work. Emotional support and appreciation are crucial as part of the "payment" and support for volunteer time and energy.

A related theme is the problem of *relationships with the professionals or supervisory staff*. Some volunteers sense that the professionals are a block to initiative and innovativeness. Others cite a lack of consultative help in critical situations and a lack of the orientaton and training they need to do the job well. Perhaps one of the most frequent and serious problems in this area is the feeling that the staff expects full commitment to their particular activity even though the volunteer may have a variety of other legitimate priorities. The staff exerts a kind of "righteous pressure" about the importance of their activity which makes the volunteer feel disloyal and guilty and hastens his withdrawal from the relationship. Closely related is the volunteer's common feeling that he is a second class citizen involved in the less important kinds of work in the program.

Another group of forces acting to decrease volunteer commitment, as seen in figure 2, centers around the volunteer's perception of *disapproval or devaluation of his commitment by others* whose opinions he values. Such forces might be the spoken or unspoken feelings of family members, the raised eyebrows of co-workers at the office, or the decision of one's service club or group to become involved in a different type of service priority. A related force is the volunteer's hesitation to become involved in an activity that may be the subject of public controversy.

Another theme seems to be the *general morale and working conditions* of the volunteer program. If there are persistent rumors that the program is regarded as unimportant and that there are budget cuts in the offing, the volunteer gets the sense of being on a sinking ship. Probably the "Situational Forces" become more of an issue when other and more central psychological factors are already fostering negative attitudes toward one's volunteer work and situation.

Turning to the positive factors pushing toward continued volunteer effort and an increase in personal commitment, we again see several clusters. One very important theme seems to be the *sense of "making a difference,"* of contributing to some significant service that changes or helps the lives of others or, in the case of a political campaign or other "cause work," the sense of being connected to or even influencing national policy or international events.

Related to the sense of the significance of their work is the volunteers' *feeling that they are appreciated* and influencing their co-workers and the job situation: that their suggestions and ideas are being used, that they are invited to join in planning and policy thinking, and that they are trusted to take on more and more responsibility.

Another important theme is the sense of *self-actualization,* of "doing one's own thing," of feeling more competent and adequate, of learning a lot and being excited about new insights, and even of transferring one's learning and experiences to other parts of one's life situation, such as one's family life.

Another theme is that *volunteers have the support of persons and groups who are important to them.* It may be expressed as being involved in the volunteer work with a friend with whom there is a lot of off-the-job sharing and discussing, as having found new friends, or as finding that one's husband, wife or teen-ager is supportive and enthusiastic about the activity. Reading articles in the mass media supporting the importance of one's voluntary effort and having one's company give public recognition to volunteer service by its employees are other important motivating forces toward legitimizing and intensifying one's commitment.

Another group of supportive forces centers around the volunteers' feelings that the organization they are working with is motivated to make *adjustments to fit their schedule* and to support their participation in every way possible—for example, by providing the place and supplies for co-workers to get together for coffee and conversation, by paying registration fees for conferences, and by reimbursing the volunteer for transportation, meals, babysitting, and necessary telephone calls.

In the next two chapters we will be examining some of the approaches and techniques that have a positive impact on the decision of the volunteer to say yes to an invitation, to become creatively involved, and continue to serve. But before turning to specifics we want to focus on one other aspect of the total context of the dynamics of motivation. As we have seen, much of the motivation and commitment of volunteers depends upon the values, attitudes, and behaviors of their professional supervisors and coordinators, and upon the policies and psychological atmosphere of the agency or organization. So, in turn, the nature of the motivation of the professional, the utilizer of volunteers, becomes a very important topic for our inquiry. What motivates the decision to seek help from volunteers, to provide attractive opportunities for them, and to give them the training and support they need on the job?

Whether and How To Use Volunteers

Although there are many trends in society and in the helping professions toward increased use of volunteer personpower, there are also a number of significant forces working against increasing the use of volunteers—in fact, even forces discouraging the use of untrained and inexperienced helpers at all, as we saw in Chapter III. In figure 3 we have summarized the psychological, interpersonal, and situational forces that motivate professional leadership to make extensive use of volunteers and, on the other hand, the factors that cause some professionals to be very cautious in recruiting volunteers and in giving them responsibility. As with figures 1 and 2, we suggest that you check figure 3 against your own experience and make additions to the force field.

Figure 3. Deciding Whether and How To Use Volunteers

Decision to use extensively at high level of responsibility	*Decision to make minimal use with limited responsibility*
Forces toward maximal use of volunteers	*Forces toward minimal use of volunteers*
─────────────────➤	◄─────────────────

Forces Inside Professional
Decision Maker ("Own Forces")

I feel need to extend service beyond what I can do	I don't want to give up the rewards of direct contact with clients
─────────────────➤	◄─────────────────
The volunteers I've worked with have been great	I am uneasy working with volunteers of different race, class, education, etc.
─────────────────➤	◄─────────────────
They are fun to train and work with	I distrust volunteers' ethical sensitivity to the need for confidentiality
─────────────────➤	◄─────────────────

They are a key link to clients →	Paraprofessionals are easier to train and control ←
The best delivery of service is by a team of volunteer, professional, and paraprofessional →	Training and supervising them will take too much time ←
There is great personal satisfaction in seeing volunteers grow as I work with them →	The volunteers might be more accepted than I am by clients ←
I can have more impact by spreading my skills →	I don't see what jobs I can give them ←
More volunteers are available to be recruited →	Too much energy is required to recruit them ←
Volunteers are ready to take more responsibility today →	They resist supervision, ignore policy, embarrass the agency ←
	I don't feel expert enough to supervise new roles and functions ←
	They just are not responsible ←

"Interpersonal and Group Member Forces"

Board says we should give more service with no more professionals →	Standards of good service are becoming more professional all the time ←
The chief executive values extensive use of volunteers →	The volunteers are too aggressive in seeking status, power, independence ←
The funding agency values our use of volunteers →	My colleagues tell me that volunteers are inadequate in many areas ←
Our agency policy is to use volunteers in many roles →	Parents are raising questions about our using volunteers ←

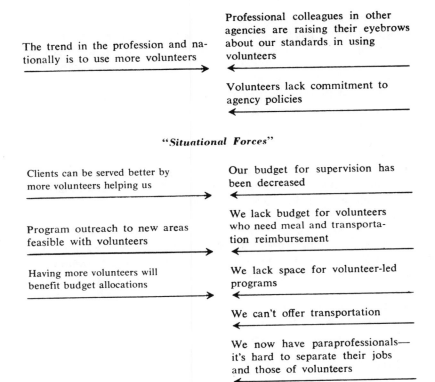

The trend in the profession and nationally is to use more volunteers →

Professional colleagues in other agencies are raising their eyebrows about our standards in using volunteers ←

Volunteers lack commitment to agency policies ←

"Situational Forces"

Clients can be served better by more volunteers helping us →

Our budget for supervision has been decreased ←

Program outreach to new areas feasible with volunteers →

We lack budget for volunteers who need meal and transportation reimbursement ←

Having more volunteers will benefit budget allocations →

We lack space for volunteer-led programs ←

We can't offer transportation ←

We now have paraprofessionals— it's hard to separate their jobs and those of volunteers ←

A number of themes of motivation emerge from figure 3 as guides to understanding the life space of the professionals and to working with them on the more effective use of volunteers. One important theme is the *rewards and personal satisfactions that come from client feedback.* There is something deeply satisfying about responses of gratitude and growth from those one is attempting to help. Some of this emotional satisfaction is admittedly lost when the professionals "let the volunteers have all the fun" while they, removed from the firing line, act as trainers, supervisors, supporters, and behind-the-scenes administrators and organizers.

A second related theme is *concern about professional standards,* about the quality of service rendered, and about the potential danger to clients from insensitive and unskilled helpers. The idea that volunteers with relatively brief training can be expected to do some of the things the professional spent years getting trained for is a threat and a source of genuine professional concern. Within their own peer group professionals share anecdotes and attitudes about the irresponsibility or unpredictability of volunteers, their ethical boners in regard to confidentiality, their ignorance of professional standards, the difficulties of training them, their resistance to supervision, and their impulsiveness in ignoring agency policies.

A third source of resistance probably is the fact that most professionals have had *no training in the techniques and skills of recruiting, training, and supervising volunteers.* They therefore lack a feeling of competence and confidence in this area. Their sense of inadequacy is increased by their awareness that indigenous volunteers have skills and knowhow that the professionals lack, and that many volunteers today have professionally trained skills from their own areas of competence which represent major resources beyond the expertness of the professional.

Another common theme is the *feeling that the need for more personpower can be better met by paraprofessionals* than by volunteers. Many professionals feel more comfortable working with, training, and supervising paid subordinates who fit right into the organizational system and are ready to take supervision as paid staff members. They feel that volunteers are much more difficult to deal with in defined role relationships, and much less predictable in terms of commitment and responsiveness to supervision.

Now it is time to look at the other half of figure 3, at the forces motivating professionals toward increased use of volunteers, at higher levels of responsibility. Needs and opportunities for helping services are expanding and will continue to intensify in the future. The *need for services* will predictably outstrip the training of professional and paraprofessional workers. The economic base will not be available for supporting the training and maintenance of enough staffs of paid workers. For these reasons, more and more agencies and professional workers are seeing the necessity of making much fuller use of volunteers in all areas of service, including some that have previously had no or few volunteer helpers, such as school systems, government offices, health services, cultural centers, food services, etc.

A second important source of motivation toward more extensive use of volunteers is the *increasing number and variety of potential volunteers.* More and more persons with highly trained skills, and with great sensitivity and commitment, are available, and often their knowledge and skills complement those of the professional.

Organizing, coordinating, and facilitating the use of these volunteer resources are very exciting challenges for professional leadership. Many professionals are discovering that the colleagueship and appreciation of volunteer co-workers can become even more rewarding than their relationships with professional colleagues or with their clients.

Another source of motivation is the realization that *reaching out to serve the populations most in need of help can be effectively accomplished only with volunteers,* because these populations cannot pay for services. Besides, professionals have been discovering that, even if the neediest communities could support fully professional services, these would not be as effective as services by teams of indigenous volunteers, because the *professionals' cultural and economic backgrounds and racial identification often make it difficult for them to connect* with these populations. Many professionals have found a new source of regard and satisfaction in spreading their professionally trained resources to the training and supporting of teams of local volunteers, who are better able to relate to their peers.

As we work toward increased use of volunteers we need to be continuously sensitive to the dilemmas and genuine problems of the professionals and their agencies. We must focus on the problems of their motivation and their future perspectives as well as on those of the volunteer, because the professionals are very much a part of the motivational dynamics of voluntarism in our society.

Generalizations

Let's pause to review some of the major generalizations about motivation that we can derive from the analysis in this chapter and the preceding ones.

Volunteer Motivation

1. A major motivating factor for volunteers is the opportunity to participate in problem solving and significant decision making.

2. The placement of volunteers should include some process for relating the type of work and situation to their particular interests, needs, and motivations.

3. To increase motivation, most volunteer opportunities should provide for both self-actualizing personal development and meaningful service to the needs of others. In other words, the opportunities for volunteer service should be presented both as continuing educational opportunities to learn and grow and as op-

portunities to contribute one's "tithe" of much-needed social service.

4. The "contract" between the volunteer and the organization should legitimize a feasible level of commitment and allow for personal variations in time, energy, and interest without guilt or tension about divided loyalties and limited energy.

5. The on-the-job experience of the volunteer should include continuing opportunities for reflective study and evaluation and for joint planning and designing of service goals and action. Much of the volunteer's sustaining and renewing motivation comes from seeing clear steps toward the group's goals and from successfully completing them one by one.

6. Needs can be met and motivation sustained more effectively if the work situation also allows for individual advancement through a series of steps leading to higher levels of responsibility, skill, learning, and influence.

7. For many volunteers motivation will be increased if a record of activities is kept, that becomes part of a resume and may lead to paid work.

8. Motivation will be sustained best if there are regular mechanisms for supportive feedback from clients, co-workers, and professional leadership, and for recognition from the agency and community.

9. Participation in meaningful training activities inside and outside the organization (e.g., conferences) is an important source of continuing motivation and growth.

Motivation of the Professional Users of Volunteers

1. The motivation of the professionals to give priority to work with volunteers will be strengthened if the agency policy makers and administrators establish a climate that shows that they value the use of volunteers and encourage the devotion of professional time to recruiting, training, coordinating, and consulting with volunteers.

2. The motivation to use volunteers will be enhanced if professional development opportunities are provided to help promote competence and confidence in the concepts and skills of recruiting, training, administering, and coordinating volunteers. Outside conferences, seminars, consultants and trainers often provide additional good resources for this training.

3. Opportunities should be provided for the professionals to discuss openly with their peers the importance and techniques of work with volunteers and to develop joint goals, plans, and commitments in this area.

4. The motivation of the professional users of volunteers will be strengthened and sustained if mechanisms for regular feedback are established to provide "appreciation data" from volunteers and from the agency.

5. Designs to get evaluation feedback from clients and client groups about the success of volunteer work will help professionals validate their decisions about the use of volunteers, improve training, and make consultative supervision more effective.

6. Professional motivation to work with volunteers will be strengthened by the establishment of regular procedures for joint study, training, planning, and evaluation by teams comprising professionals, paraprofessionals, and volunteers. These sessions should include sensitivity learning process work on communication, interpersonal feelings, and problems of working relationships.

7. Professionals will be more motivated to work with volunteers if time and money is budgeted for them to be able to do so.

V Recruitment and Orientation

Creative use of volunteers is closely related to an effective recruitment and orientation process, linking a person who wants to give time and energy to an organization that needs volunteers in order to operate; linking a need for self-actualization with an opportunity for experience; linking a need to learn with opportunities for learning; linking a need to be creative with an opportunity to give the most creative service possible. Through this linkage (recruitment) the potential volunteer becomes an actual service and decision making agent. As the person becomes part of the agency, he/she links the agency to the client and the community. Because the very basis of volunteer service is built at the time the potential volunteer is first recruited, the recruitment process is crucially important.

Preliminary Considerations

The process of recruitment must be thought through and planned very carefully. In locating and attracting "linker-volunteers" an organization should first examine closely its need for volunteers and the special resources, skills and values they bring. A recruiting organization needs to be very clear about the kinds of jobs and tasks that need doing and about the kinds of volunteers who can do them best. Too often the motivations and needs of the organization are not clearly communicated to the potential volunteer.

The second requirement for an organization hoping to link volunteer resources into its service system is to take time to understand what kinds of motivations, needs, and interests each potential volunteer has, so as to match these with the kinds of service opportunities available. Does the potential volunteer feel a need for meaningful involvement in giving service? Or is the motivation a need for self-actualization and for new growth and learning experiences? One volunteer's main interest might be in making good use of special interests or competencies. Another might wish to serve in a particular organization because of the cause it represents. Cause motivation is very important in this day of social revolution. Many volunteers want to be where the action is and where they feel their time and energy will make a difference.

One can also look at volunteers in terms of the kind of service they give. Some give direct service: tutoring, helping patients in a hospital, leading a youth group, working with the mentally retarded, soliciting funds, getting out the vote, training others in a particular skill. Other volunteers do administrative work. Often these are persons who have had previous experience, although this is not necessary, in order to sit on a board or committee and help the organization make its policy and action decisions. The administrative jobs include both those to which volunteers are elected for a certain period of time and those to which they are appointed on an ad hoc basis to complete a particular project, such as revising bylaws.

Where To Find Potential Volunteers

There are, of course, many different kinds of organizations looking for volunteers: private volunteer agencies such as hospitals and scout groups; public agencies such as departments of welfare, mental health, and education; political and cause groups. The easiest and probably most popular way to recruit new volunteers is through those who are already in a given organization and are having a good experience there. They then act as "referral linkers." Some organizations recruit volunteers through the volunteer bureau in their community. Sometimes potential volunteers present themselves on their own initiative. Newcomers to an area, for example, often volunteer their services in hopes of becoming a part of the community more quickly. People wanting to serve in poverty areas also frequently volunteer on their own initiative. Sometimes there is group motivation: a small group of members of another organization volunteer to serve together to carry out a certain task. Many people, particularly teenagers and senior citizens, feel more secure if they are able to volunteer and serve with at least one friend. Some volunteers can be recruited only through personal contact. Others respond to ads in newspapers or on radio or television. Because different people can be reached by different recruitment techniques, organizations seeking volunteers should employ the widest possible range of techniques and try to learn more about when to use which ones.

Over the years, most of the volunteers recruited by most agencies have been middle or upper-middle class white women. Only recently has there been an attempt to draw volunteers from the poorer sectors of the community. This shift has been spearheaded by cause movements, political organizations, and public agencies, and through such legislation as the Economic Opportunity Act. The challenge to all agencies, organizations, and movements is to find the important underutilized volunteer resources in areas that have not previously been tapped. New recruiting methods are having to be developed, since new volunteers often cannot be found through the traditional methods. The only people who can be recruited through established agencies, for example, are those who are already connected in some way to these organizations.

To find potential volunteers who are not members of establishment organizations or groups, recruiters are going to such places as *laundromats, bowling alleys, street corner clubs, neighborhood ice cream or hamburger spots, adult education classes, Americanization classes, Job Corps and Head Start centers, post offices, pool halls,* and *informal neighborhood social groups.* Recruiters have also discovered the possibilities of *supermarket bulletin boards, merchants associations, labor unions,* and *neighborhood improvement clubs.* The *waiting rooms of public health and housing centers, welfare and probation departments,* and *other public service agencies* are particularly good places to recruit previously untapped volunteers.

"Informants" who can help find volunteers include the *mailman,* the *numbers man,* the local *bartender,* the local *police,* especially those who still walk a beat, *adult education teachers, elementary and secondary school teachers and principals, clergymen, public health doctors and nurses, neighborhood market owners, liquor store owners, gas station attendants, bus drivers* on regular routes, *barbers, beauticians,* and *older citizens* who have lived in the area for a long time. *Social workers, antipoverty workers, probation and parole officers, directors of public housing and community centers,* and *all other public service personnel,* including volunteers and paraprofessionals, also make good "informants" about potential volunteers.

The main thing to remember is that people know other people, who need only to be asked. It has become very clear that most people are eager to participate as volunteers, if they are just given the opportunity.

Types of Volunteers

Volunteers can be found with almost every possible combination of age, sex, race, education, religion, experience, and life-style. There are the very young (e.g., nine- and ten-year-olds) tutoring the even younger. There are teen-age volunteers like the Candy Stripers in hospitals. There are the brand new volunteers who may not even be familiar with the concept of volunteering, and the experienced volunteers whose previous work may or may not be relevant to their new job. (It is important to make no assumptions about how much a potential volunteer knows or has done. The recruiter should ask the persons about previous volunteer work, both what they did and how they felt about it.)

The history of voluntarism shows that traditionally there have been many more jobs for women than for men. Indeed there are some stereotypes in the volunteer world: for example, writers routinely refer to the volunteer as *she.* However, there are just as many interesting opportunities for male volunteers, such as work in museums and as Big Brothers and scout leaders.

Matching the Recruitment Technique to the Volunteer

Once a potential volunteer has expressed interest in learning more about the opportunities with a particular organization, the recruiter must choose the most appropriate place to meet with the volunteer. Possibilities include the applicant's home or school, the local meeting spot, the recruiting organization's office, or any other place designated by the applicant. If the volunteer must travel a long distance to meet the recruiter, it helps to have the organization reimburse transportation expenses. Often the recruiter can meet the applicant halfway, or even pick her/him up at home. "Car chats" are a great way to begin recruitment and orientation.

The recruiter can meet the prospective volunteer alone or with another recruiter. Pairs of recruiters often give each other the necessary support and courage to do the recruitment job. Another technique is to bring groups of potential volunteers together. For example, 10 girls wanting to tutor in the same school were invited to a "coke hour discussion" where they talked over what they wanted to do and what the opportunities for them would be. Still another useful recruitment method is to invite the potential volunteer to participate in some ongoing activity of the organization and so get a feeling for what it is about.

Offering the Opportunity Effectively

It is important that the potential volunteers perceive the opportunity they are being offered as interesting and worthwhile. The following are some of the techniques that may be especially helpful here:

- In a warm, personal telephone call make a date to see the applicant at a mutually convenient time and place. (Often it helps to go to the potential volunteers' home rather than ask them to come to an office.)
- Send a handwritten note inviting them to a meeting of potential volunteers or to an appointment with the recruiter.
- Have someone the prospective volunteers know approach them personally on a one-to-one basis.
- Allow for immediate sign-up after presenting to a group the kinds of volunteer opportunities available, so the potential volunteers will feel that they are really wanted and that there is an organization ready to receive them.
- Have the particular client group needing volunteers recruit directly. For example, teen-age groups needing an adult sponsor or resource person often do a better job recruiting their own volunteers than could be done through the general recruiting efforts of the larger agency or organization.
- Seize the right moment, such as a chat at the market where a person shows interest, or after a community meeting in which someone's interest has been expressed.
- Invite the potential volunteer to visit the organization's headquarters. Let them meet other volunteers already on the job, perhaps over lunch or coffee, so they can discuss what they are doing and how they feel about it. Introduce them to some of the professionals on the staff. Here is an opportunity for the potential recruit to get the feel of how the professionals see themselves in relationship to volunteers.
- Involve the potential volunteers in an activity without committing them to it. For instance, 13 poverty-area volunteers were invited to visit the pediatrics department of a local hospital, where they had the opportunity to see how patients were treated and to ask questions of doctors, nurses, patients, and the clerical and custodial help; they then reconvened a week later to talk about what they might like to do as volunteers in that setting.
- Use personal follow-up. This may mean telephoning to see how the person feels about the opportunity a week later, or it may

mean a warm personal letter, a coffee hour, or a home visit. Whatever the method, follow-up is a crucial factor in attracting the potential volunteer.

- Encourage prospective volunteers to state their needs, interests, and expectations. It is important that people who are about to donate their time to an organization be given an opportunity to ask all the questions they have and to think over how and when they might best serve and with whom they would like to work.
- Use attractive literature to interpret the organization's work. It is better to use one snappy, interesting, clearly written piece than to overwhelm the applicant with packets and packets of materials, most of which make better sense to the already indoctrinated person than to one who knows very little or nothing about the organization's purposes and services.
- Give the volunteer a choice of jobs. Rarely do people fit into jobs; rather, jobs must be molded to the interests and resources of the individual. Job descriptions should be flexible or nonexistent. It is sometimes best for new volunteers to be able to carve out their jobs and then write their job descriptions after several weeks of experience.
- Allow for a period of orientation. This gives the volunteers a change to get used to the job before they commit themselves to long-term service. It also helps to offer short-term possibilities for service, so that volunteers can contribute time and energy without necessarily signing up for three years.

These, then, are some of the ways to attract volunteers—to ensure that potential volunteers will decide to become active volunteers.

Orientation

Orientation really begins with the very first contact between the potential volunteer and a representative of the recruiting organization. Often recruiters are not aware that they are in fact orienting the potential volunteer by means of the very role and behavior they model. Further orientation, of course, comes through more structured training sessions before the new recruit begins work. Orienting new volunteers means making sure that they become acquainted with the new setting and its life-styles and with the possibilities of their services' making a difference to the total life of the organization as well as to themselves.

Often new, enthusiastic volunteers are the best persons to orient the next wave of new volunteers, because they are still close to what it feels like to be new and yet just enough ahead to be able to tell them a little bit about the opportunities in store for them. There should be a variety of beginning orientation activities, matched to the needs of the volunteer who is young, middle-aged, older, new to volunteering, new to the agency, or experienced in volunteering in other settings. Orientation may continue over the first several weeks or months of service in order to give the new recruit the necessary help and support to do the job.

Retention

It should be clear that how volunteers are recruited and oriented has much to do with the enthusiasm with which they begin their service and the length of time, barring other factors, they remain in the service of a given organization. What are some of the steps an organization can take to build upon successful processes of recruitment and orientation, to ensure that new volunteers will have long, happy and successful periods of service?

1. It is helpful to draw up an individualized plan for the volunteer's on-the-job training, including personal contacts, on-the-job support, and literature that will be particularly relevant.

2. It is becoming increasingly necessary for organizations to provide in their budgets for the reimbursement of volunteers for travel, luncheons, parking, conference registrations, materials and other such items, so that the volunteers who do not have great means will be able to give of their resources, ideas, time, and service.

3. Offering a variety of jobs, opportunities for change and growth in each, and the chance to move from one job to another, or perhaps to have two jobs at once if they are ambidextrous enough, are important factors in keeping volunteers interested and motivated.

4. It is helpful for an organization to have a place for volunteers to meet together socially. This is not to say that staff members cannot go there also, but, if feasible, some kind of volunteer lounge or talk room is highly desirable.

5. Ongoing reciprocal evaluation is very valuable. It is important for volunteers to hear how well they are doing their jobs, to be able to tell the supervisor or consultant how they feel about the service they are giving, and to suggest ways in which they feel the agency could be made a better place in which to work. Identifying needs and wishes of volunteers and finding ways to meet them are helpful in establishing and keeping good volunteer-professional relationships.

6. Finding or creating new areas of service for volunteers can be

challenging to volunteers and professionals alike. Often it is the volunteers who come up with the best suggestions for new service, decision making, catalyst, or change agent roles.

7. Commitments for training and support must be made by both the volunteers and the person with whom they work. Through in-service training the volunteers can learn and grow on the job. Also, the better trained the volunteers are, the more effective the service they can render—and the more secure they will feel about the service they are giving.

Conclusion

We have seen that the world of voluntarism in the United States is experiencing some massive changes. These changes necessitate new techniques and new procedures to find, recruit, select, place, orient, and train volunteers. A new look at in-service training must also be taken. Mobility of job ladders within an organization or between organizations must be developed. Evaluation, quality control, horizontal referral and linkage, separation, termination or graduation, awards and procedures for recognition—all are functions requiring innovation and creative utilization of the resources that are available. So far most organizations and agencies do very little to help each other in such areas as the finding of underutilized segments of the population. Little has been done in interagency cooperation for the purpose of volunteer orientation and training. The changing world of voluntarism demands new action in these directions.

VI Continuous Training for Self-Renewal

If organizations are to be viable, they must have an ongoing training plan for self-renewal. Commitment to the self-renewal and agency-renewal ideal implies that plans will be translated into action and that the organization will be flexible enough to change plans when better ones are found and to fit plans to people, rather than the reverse.

An ideal continuous training plan might have five phases, as follows:

1. *Preservice training,* that is, training of a volunteer before beginning work.

2. *Start-up support,* that is assistance to the volunteers as they begin their volunteer work. Here the trainer may well be another volunteer who has had some experience in the organization and on the job.

3. *Maintenance-of-effort training.* Throughout the volunteer's period of service regular times are needed for asking questions and gaining additional job related knowledge. The volunteer needs to feel that the organization is committed to growth on the job.

4. *Periodic review and feedback.* Frequently in the beginning, probably less often as time goes on, the trainer or supervisor and the volunteer need to have the opportunity, either in a face-to-face conference or in a group meeting, to discuss whether goals are being accomplished, how the volunteer feels about accomplishment, feels about the organization, how the job and service could be improved, and how the trainer feels the volunteer could function more efficiently, and so on.

5. *Transition training.* As we have stressed elsewhere in this volume, volunteers have a need to grow and to assume more responsibility. In order to really enjoy their job they must take on additional tasks in that job or see that it can lead to additional or alternative avenues of service. This need is so often forgotten.

Why, for instance, don't organizations plan explicitly to train potential chairmen, presidents, and coordinators? If transition training were given, it would not be nearly so difficult to find new people to take over leadership, because they would have been groomed for that kind of responsibility.

This ideal framework, then, provides, for the self-renewal of the agency, as well as the volunteer. Let us examine a little more closely each of its phases.

Preservice Training

Preservice training helps the new volunteer take a look at self and skills, at the job that needs to be done, and at the organization's philosophy and services. It may be given individually or in a group setting, depending of course on the timing, the number of volunteers, and the kinds of resources and facilities available.

Preservice training actually begins with the recruitment process. At the very first contact with an individual or group, some unconscious training usually takes place. It can be made even more effective if the recruiter becomes consciously aware that as the volunteers are being acquainted with the organization's program and philosophy, they are being trained.

One thing that should definitely be included in preservice training is a tour of the organization's headquarters or the site of its services. It is important for the potential volunteer to gain an understanding of the operation of the organization through structured observation. If a trainer or guide is not available for the tour, it is possible to use a "taped-tour master" (like those in museums) to guide the volunteer through the site, pointing out the stop points, stop action points, and discussion and observation points and suggesting things to read in the library. The volunteer might be given a schedule of the staff meetings and other meetings to attend, suggesting things to look and listen for in them. Opportunities for informal chats with other volunteers and staff during coffee or lunch hours should also be built into the tour. At its conclusion, there should be time for the volunteer to discuss observations and reactions with some staff members or volunteer trainers who have been assigned to the preservice training process. There might even be a group discussion with staff, board members, potential volunteers, and active volunteers and trainers all participating. At some point in the preservice period the volunteer should meet, either formally or informally, all the kinds of people involved in the service of the organization, including paraprofessionals and clients.

Another way to conduct preservice training is through "apprenticeship observation." That is, the potential volunteer works briefly with staff or experienced volunteers in a variety of jobs around the organization so that one can make a more informed choice of work preferences.

Certainly group meetings are vital in the preservice period. Potential volunteers must be given a chance to talk with one another and to hear each other's questions and ideas, but it is equally important that they receive some conceptual input from a person representing the organization. Most potential volunteers need help in clarifying their future roles or in understanding other people's roles.

They usually also need some anticipatory practice, some role playing to help confront what it means to enter a system as a new person. To assure a smooth start when they begin their jobs, these role-playing sessions might include practice in such things as how to greet the clients of the organization, how to work with the supervisor, how to use the telephone effectively—whatever is appropriate for the kinds of jobs the volunteers will be assuming.

Preservice training, then is a vitally important part of the continuous training framework. So often the beginning steps are either taken too fast or entirely overlooked, and yet this initial training provides the very foundation for later service and contribution by the volunteers.

Start-Up Training

When the volunteer, having had some initial training, begins actual work for the organization, one enters a period in which much support is needed. Beginnings are hard for all of us. The whole period of testing out and getting acquainted, leading hopefully toward mutual trust and acceptance, is a very difficult one. But it is also a fruitful period of training, because there is in the new volunteer, as in the child, greater openness to change at the beginning than after patterns have developed.

The start-up is the time when the volunteer's repertoire of resources, skills, and alternatives is probably least developed. One therefore finds decision making difficult and needs particular help in this area. The volunteer in the start-up period also has a great need to feel recognized and accepted by the people already in the system. They must somehow communicate that they want and need volunteers, depend on their resources to extend their own services, and are really glad to have them aboard.

How can this kind of start-up support be given? There are a number of ways. One is for the supervisor, trainer, co-worker to have a supportive chat, either in person or on the telephone, with the volunteer after the first day on the job, to ask how things went and what kinds of feelings and questions there might be, and to share observations about performance, particularly positive and supportive ones. An alternative method is to have each new volunteer paired with a more experienced volunteer or a staff member from the very beginning. The pair goes through the job the first day together and then discusses what each of them observed and experienced. If the number of new volunteers is not too large, it is possible to continue the use of these pairs throughout the start-up period, with the more experienced partner acting as ongoing trainer and consultant, and the new volunteer feeling free to talk either in person or on the telephone at any needed time. (Good places that are often overlooked for these talks are the car, the airplane, the traveling bus. It is possible to use the time spent going from one place to another, even going from the organization to lunch and back for productive chats. One might say that we need to develop our "car consultant skill.")

Another way to help at the beginning is to have a short meeting of the new volunteers at which they reflect together on what's happened, how they feel about it, and to what degree they think they have accomplished the tasks set before them. Their trainer should be present to provide answers and feedback. An "open clinic" can also be held at the home of one of the volunteers to discuss their new experience. If there is a large group, discussions and problem clinics can be held weekly throughout the start-up period, to give support to all the newcomers together.

A different method sometimes found useful in start-up training is to place the volunteer in a variety of spots with experienced people so that, early in their career, they will understand not only their own job but also those of other staff and volunteers.

Yet another alternative for start-up training might be for volunteers to tape their own work and then, at the end of the day or the end of several periods of work, to listen to the tape with a helper (a co-volunteer, the consultant, a trainer, or the supervisor), discussing how each situation might have been handled differently.

Maintenance-of-Effort Training

The purposes of on-the-job training are to increase the skill of volunteers, to get them out of any ruts they might have fallen into, to answer questions and deal with concerns, to refine practices. In short, it is the meat of the training once the volunteer has become a part of the system. As good morale does not necessarily come of its own accord, on-the-job training may also be seen as a means of building and maintaining morale. Much of this training is given informally and irregularly by the supervisor or consultant, but there should also be a plan for some formal training sessions, whether workshops or individual sessions. The plan should, of course, be flexible and subject to change.

What kinds of maintenance-of-effort training are useful? There can be regular co-volunteer meetings at which volunteers interview each other about their jobs and discuss their new knowledge, resources, and questions. Sometimes at these meetings they can be asked to fill out "self-reflection sheets," indicating how they feel about the job they are doing and the people they are working with, how they would change the organization if they could, and so forth. These self-reflection sheets can then serve as the basis for group discussion and even for suggestions for new practices within the organization.

Input sessions are another kind of maintenance-of-effort training. In these sessions new plans or procedures or research findings are shared with the volunteers, or additional information about a particular volunteer job or function is given to further their growth. Volunteers can also attend staff meetings as part of their on-the-job training. Such attendance should be carefully planned beforehand, some kind of observation or listening guide should be provided to the volunteers, and there should be full discussion afterwards. The content of the staff meetings chosen should, of course, be relevant to the volunteers' jobs and interests.

Another important part of on-the-job training is making time available periodically for the volunteers to read new resource or program material. Most organizations receive and send out many, many materials, such as staff speeches, government pamphlets, films, etc., but these are rarely available to volunteers. There should also be an opportunity for volunteers to meet the new resource people who have entered the system.

Regular problem clinics are an important part of many on-the-job training programs. Sometimes particular kinds of training arise out of these clinics. For instance, in one agency volunteers were having a hard time connecting with the very young clients. After this problem came out at a problem clinic, a series of meetings with young people was set up to look at how such connecting could be done more skillfully.

On-the-job training can also take the form of an "exchange of practices institute" at which people with similar jobs in different organizations get together to share practices and innovations they have developed. For instance, teachers and teacher aides from several school systems can meet to discuss how they build their teacher–teacher aide team and what kinds of things each half of the team likes to do.

Another idea is to give the volunteers a "mini-sabbatical"— perhaps a month off to "travel" in their community to other sites similar to their own to get ideas, or to take a training seminar during the hours in which they would usually be offering service. This kind of renewal has not previously been considered for volunteers, but it is very important if they are to continue to give productive, efficient, and innovative service in a job they have held for any period of time.

Surely the volunteer staff of any organization should be apprised of what is available to them in nearby college and extension and adult education courses. Often there are some very relevant courses that an organization could encourage its volunteers to take, perhaps by reimbursing their tuition. A recent example is a course at the University of California in Riverside called "New Skills for People Helpers." This was a one-day workshop in which the participants and consultants looked at the new trends affecting people helpers and at the ways in which they needed to refine and add to their skills. The interaction of people from a variety of organizations and the exchange of practices that took place both formally and informally that day were extremely valuable. The participants became acquainted with resources in their own community that they had not known existed.

Periodic Review and Feedback

Many types of review sessions for volunteers have been used over the years. One new method is to have the volunteer and the consultant each tape record in a soliloquy some of their observations about what they feel is being done well and what could be improved, along with any other comments they wish to make to one another. They then listen to each other's tapes and prepare for a face-to-face discussion of their content.

Another new technique is to video tape a volunteer's work periodically, allowing them to look at their own practice and analyze shortcomings. They can then help determine the kind of training they need most. It is also wise to consult the organization's clients in planning training for the volunteers. They can recommend the kind of training they think will get them better service.

Whatever kind of training is used, it is important to plan for implementation of new suggestions and feedback along the way. The implementation plan ought to include some checkpoints or stop action periods where discussion can be held about how well the implementation is working out and what new problems have come up. Feedback from all sources should be taken into consideration in deciding whether to continue with or redesign any training program. Feedback cuts across all phases of training, from preservice to transition training.

Transition Training

A volunteer must be helped to move to levels of greater responsibility, whether in the present job or a new one. Just as when first coming aboard the organization, so in moving to a different job, one must be prepared for entry and must be helped to look ahead rather than back. If there are new role responsibilities, these need to be delineated through discussion, observation, role playing, interview, or in some other way. It cannot be assumed that because a person has functioned well at one level they will necessarily function equally well at the next. Transition training, therefore, whether it takes individual or group form, should recapitulate the first four phases of the training framework, in a somewhat different manner. That is, there should be pretransition training (a period of referral if the volunteer is going to be working with different people), start-up training in the new job, maintenance-of-effort training, and periodic review and feedback sessions. We have here then a circle, a framework for continuous training for self-renewal.

Some Assumptions

We now want to list some generalizations about volunteers that have important implications for their training.

1. Volunteers bring with them a wide variation of experiences, knowledge, and skills. *Implication*: Training methods that build on and use the volunteer's experience, knowledge, and skills will produce the best and most relevant kind of learning.

2. Volunteers, by and large, will come as self-directed, motivated, interested learners. *Implication*: Volunteers should help plan and conduct their own learning experiences as active participants rather than as passive recipients.

3. Volunteers participate in training events because they want to learn to do their volunteer jobs. *Implication*: The training must be practical and relevant to the learners and must be related to life as they know it.

4. Many volunteers will have been exposed to classroomlike learning situations that were not helpful, relevant, or exciting. *Implication*: The learning activities must take place in an informal, experiential atmosphere.

5. Volunteers have a number of important roles (as parents, workers, students, citizens) that compete for their time. *Implication*: Training should be planned to take into consideration the limited time available to most volunteers and to accept the legitimacy of their other loyalties.

6. The world of voluntarism has not developed norms or procedures to support and reward participation in ongoing training programs. *Implication*: Training opportunities and activities must be a rewarding and recognized aspect of organizational functioning.

7. Often the training format and content have been developed over the years and have not been revised or retailored for the particular participants at a particular time. *Implication:* Each training event, if possible, should be planned by trainers and some of the potential participants to meet the current needs of a particular group.

8. Training is often a one-time thing instead of an ongoing

support opportunity for volunteers. *Implication:* Ongoing, in-service training is necessary for volunteers, and the importance of follow-up should be communicated at the beginning of the learning experience.

9. Volunteer training is usually seen as an event sponsored by one organization, or for volunteers in one category, such as new, experienced, board, office workers, service personnel, etc. *Implication:* Training should be planned interorganizationally to utilize all the possible resources. Also, it should be seen in the context of a group process and of team relationships.

Determining Training Needs

The type of volunteer training depends on the agency's or organization's needs as well as on the needs and resources of the volunteers. It must be sculptured to fit a particular situation and particular people. Important variables to be taken into consider-ation in developing training plans include the amount of time volunteers will devote to the activity, their values and life style, the job to be done, the volunteers' express needs, the amount of ex-perience they have had in other relevant situations, the agency philosophy about training, the organizational goals, the consul-tant's or supervisor's or trainer's suggestions, the ongoing feed-back, and past experience. Who determines the training needs? It may be a variety of people: the recruiter or interviewer (who may be a professional, a paraprofessional, or another volunteer), a supervisor or consultant working with the volunteers, the volun-teers themselves, or the clients, who have implicitly or explicitly expressed some needs that are not now being met.

Training Models

One model for training is the workshop on a particular topic, such as how to communicate better, or how to have more pro-ductive committee meetings, or how to keep a board from get-ting bored. Such workshops might last anywhere from two to six hours and might be held two or three times a year as a result of determining some special needs. They could be led by a consul-tant, by an inside-outside change agent, or by trainers and volun-teers as a team within the organization. Another model for training is the weekend laboratory, where a group of volunteers and some specialized resource people go away for a weekend and work on a particular series of content items, such as entry into a system, how to cause change to happen in a community, or effective alternatives for conflict utilization.

Still another method of training is to hold "simulation hours," in which participants simulate situations that have occurred or are anticipated, such as the first confrontation of new youth board members with older, more experienced board members at a board meeting. Another possibility is to use confrontation designs. The confrontation can be either role-played on the spot or watched on film. One national youth-serving organization recently developed 45-second to 5-minute filmed confrontations between young and old, white and black, and other conflicting groups. At the end of each confrontation the trainees were asked to discuss what they would do at that point, sometimes taping their responses, having them evaluated by uncommitted observers, and trying again until they had developed a repertoire of alternatives for dealing with the confrontation.

Role playing is another method that can be used as part of either a workshop or a total training piece. For instance, in a recent workshop, teachers were asked to play the role of teenagers, and vice versa, for a period of time. A great deal of learning can come out of such role reversal.

Conferences bringing together organizational staff and volunteers are another training model. Volunteers and professionals from hospital settings, for example, can get together to discuss common problems, ideas, and innovative practices. The results of their meeting can then be disseminated to all those in similar jobs who could not participate in the conference.

The variety of training models is endless. The important things are that there be as many volunteers involved in the designing of these models as possible and that all alternative possibilities be looked at before a final design is drawn up. So often we rely on models that have worked in the past. By this time, however, they may be dried and true rather than tried and true, or they may not even still be true at all. Each training design should be a package unto itself, designed for a particular group or individual at a particular time for a specified purpose.

VII The Training of Trainers

As we saw in the preceding chapter, the training of volunteer manpower for the many different volunteer roles is an exciting and varied job that calls for a number of basic competencies in the trainer. These competencies do not emerge automatically from a combination of experience as a volunteer or professional practitioner and motivation to be a trainer. The skills of trainership must be learned, just as the skills of effective volunteer activity must be learned.

Probably one of the most serious barriers to the development of a high quality of voluntarism in any agency or community is the lack of available training for trainers. In this chapter we want to focus on the development of the personnel and learning activities needed for an effective "training-of-trainers" program. We will start by examining a few assumptions about the job of training trainers. Then we will look at some of the dimensions of training competence needed to be an effective trainer of volunteers, of volunteer-paraprofessional-professional teams, and of units of volunteers such as boards, committees, and action groups. Next we will describe several approaches to achieving competence as a trainer-of-trainers. Finally we will look at an illustrative program for the professional development of trainers and supervisors of volunteers.

Some Initial Assumptions and Propositions

Being a very competent trainer of volunteers is not adequate preparation for being a good trainer of other trainers, because the training of trainers is a different type of task requiring different competencies from those involved in direct training and supervising of volunteers. Therefore, every organization or community using volunteer personpower needs to develop special trainership resources to provide a continuing program for the training of trainers.

The training of teams, groups, and total organizations is different from the training of individual volunteers. Because group training is an important trend in the training of volunteers, it is necessary to provide opportunities to learn this type of trainership skill.

Since at present there are relatively few well qualified trainers-of-trainers in any local community, it is desirable for agencies and organizations to collaborate in developing and using personnel who are qualified to function as trainers-of-trainers.

New models and materials for training are developing very rapidly, so it is important to provide continuing "renewal opportunities" for the personnel who are involved in the training of trainers.

Because almost all training programs require a creative integration of substantive content knowledge and process or procedural learnings, the programs for the training of trainers, rather than focusing just on process learning (such as sensitivity training by itself) or just on content learning (such as the substantive knowledge and skills of a particular agency program content), need to emphasize the skills of integrating these two forms of learning.

Trainership requires both diagnostic sensitivity to the training needs of the different types of trainees and skill in deriving creative training designs to meet them. This dual requirement has very important implications for the training designs for the training of trainers.

The implications of these assumptions will be seen in the remaining sections of this chapter.

Elements of Competent Trainership That Need To Be Taught

Skill in Diagnosing Needs, Readiness, and Potential for Learning. A core area of competence for all trainers is the skillful diagnosis of the situations of their trainee clients. The trainer must learn what kind of information can and must be collected ahead of time, before training activities begin, and what kind needs to be collected continuously in order to develop training designs to meet developing needs and changing readiness in the learners. Learning how to collect information and to think diagnostically about each individual trainee, or about subgroups of trainees who are significantly different in their levels of skills and readiness, is difficult. But an even more exciting challenge is learning to become diagnostic about the total client system of which the trainee is a part—to be diagnostic about total groups or organizations as the clients of training activity.

A basic distinction in diagnostic orientation and technique is between discovering the "here and now pains" which are motivating an individual or a group to desire some kind of change and getting diagnostic information about the "images of potentiality" that exist for individuals or groups. These images can provide the basis for the development of objectives and motivations for growth.

One of the trainer's most important skills is that of involving the trainees in the diagnostic process: helping them clarify their own learning needs, set learning goals, and begin to work collaboratively on the learning activities for meeting those goals. Probably two of the greatest weaknesses in the training of volunteers are (a) the preparation of training designs and materials without involving the learner-volunteers in the diagnosis of need and readiness and (b) the lack of planning to provide different learning opportunities for trainees who are at different levels of experience and different states of development of their skills, attitudes, and values as volunteer workers.

A guidesheet for thinking about client needs, and about developing a plan for training, and a design for specific training sessions has been prepared by the authors.[1]

Competence in Macrodesigning. Most trainers have little opportunity to develop competence and flexibility in designing total learning experiences for a group of trainees. Usually the most important decisions about a training program, i.e., decisions about the overall design of the training activity, are made without exploring a number of alternative designs and without keeping in mind the many clear guidelines that maximize the probability of high quality learning experiences for all trainees. Here are a few of these guidelines:

- The design must support internalization and application of learning by providing opportunities for each trainee to connect within self new information acquired, to evaluate the relevance of

[1]"Designing Learning Experiences Planning Charts", Organization Renewal, Inc., Washington, D.C., 1973.

that information to self, to develop intentions to use in action the implications of the information, to plan, to act, and to develop skills to carry out action intentions.

- The design should confront learners with situations which require them to make decisions and to act, rather than just to observe or "think about things."
- The training design should enable the learners to work on the transfer of their learnings from the training situation to the real-life situations in which they will be expected to apply them.
- To the degree possible, the training design needs to provide for the development of relationships between trainees which will have support value after the training is completed. In many training situations there are two or more persons from the same setting, or persons who will be working in the same area. The training design should provide opportunities to develop collaborative teamwork and joint planning for future support on the job, where the volunteers will be facing the risks of playing for keeps and will be in critical need of support.
- The training design must provide for appropriate individualization of learning opportunities, rather than push all learners into conformity to one pattern.
- The training design must allow for progressive degrees of involvement of the trainees in the planning and execution of their own learning activities and learning design so that they can become increasingly independent of the trainer and increasingly competent in taking the initiative.
- The design must take into account the overall purposes, structures, and programs of the agencies and organizations from which the learners come so that there is optimal linkage between the learning activities of the training program and the application-of-learning situations with which the trainees will be coping.
- The macrodesign must carefully consider the time and facilities available for training, the structure of the situation in which the training will take place, the possible types of groupings of trainees, the division of labor among trainers, the mix of individual and group work time, and the balance of work and recreation.

The authors have presented guidelines and examples of macrodesigning in their Chapter "Designing for Participative

Learning and Changing", in the new volume: Benne, Bradford, Gibb and Lippitt, THE LABORATORY METHOD OF LEARN-ING AND CHANGING: THEORY AND APPLICATION, Science and Behavior Books, Palo Alto, Calif., 1975.

Competence in Microdesigning. A microdesign is a plan for a single session or several sessions that fit into the overall macro-design. Some microdesigns are focused primarily on opportunities for skill practice, others for conceptualization, others for work on back-home application or for any of the other functions that are components of the total learning program. In order to be flexible and creative a trainer needs to be able to retrieve from own ex-peience and that of others a variety of microdesign alternatives to meet a particular training objective.

For example, after considering all the diagnostic information one has available about a new group of trainees, the trainer needs to be able to create a "start-up design" which will relate to people where they are and help them get started on the learning pro-gram. Sometimes the effective start-up is a microlab session that gives the trainees a brief taste of the various kinds of learning activities they will be experiencing in the total training program. Sometimes it is important to work through a sharing of the trainer's and trainees' expectations for the whole training activity, to develop a mutually understood "contract for teaching and learning." Some-times a confrontation problem to be solved is the appropriate start-up.

Another type of microdesign is aimed at providing the trainees with "conceptual input," i.e., some concepts and principles which will help them develop comprehension of their roles as volunteers and of the processes of interaction involved in helping others. Most trainers have discovered that giving a lecture is not the way to help learners develop an understanding of basic concepts. But very few trainers have been helped to discover and try out the many alternatives to a didactic presentation.

The skill-practice exercise is another important kind of micro-design. The authors have presented an analysis of types of skill practice training and designs in a recent publication.[2] All trainers

[2]"Awareness Learning and Skill Development", Bradford, Benne, Gibb and Lippitt R., THE LABORATORY METHOD OF LEARNING AND CHANGING: THEORY AND AP-PLICATION, Science and Behavior Books, Palo Alto, Calif., 1975.

need to be helped to develop a library of these exercises which they can adapt to the needs of any group of learners or any individual learner. A new outstanding collection of training exercises is available.[3] The development of actual behavioral skill is one of the crucial aspects of any training program, but skill-practice opportunities represent a remarkably small portion of most training designs.

Another key aspect of good training designs is the provision for activities that help the trainee think through the application of learnings to a variety of practical situations to be faced in on-the-job settings. Planning and practicing for application and arriving at commitments to try out are key elements of the training design and require specific types of microdesign sessions.

Other elements that belong in every training design and that call for the planning of specific kinds of sessions include the provision for feedback from the learners to the trainers, to permit the learners to influence and steer the training program in terms of their own learning needs and experiences; the use of resource persons in effective ways; the retrieval and use of written resources; meditation periods for personal integration of learning; team development of learners from the same back-home situation; and the exploration of value dilemmas and ethical problems.

Often in a team of trainers we find some who are more competent in creating overall designs for learning programs and sequences and others who are more creative in the specifics of planning and executing the microdesigns for the individual sessions that make up the program. It is important for every trainer to develop both types of resourcefulness, as well as competence in diagnosis.

Skill in Making Intervention Decisions. Most trainers have remarkably little opportunity to practice, in "not playing for keeps" situations, the actual skills of interaction with trainees. Early in their experience as trainers, most professionals develop a certain style of intervention, or way of looking at the training situation, which they find successful. They continue to use this style of interaction and initiative as a trainer without much opportunity to expand their repertoire and to explore new ways of behaving. For example, many trainers tend to see the activities in the training group in terms of whether the right *content* is

[3]Research and Development, National Council of YMCAs, *Training Volunteer Leaders*, YMCA, New York, N.Y., 1974.

being learned; others tend to focus on *individual trainees* who
seem to have certain types of problems or need certain kinds
of help; still others focus on the *total learning group* and its procedures, its development, and its process issues. It is important
that every trainer be helped to develop a "trifocal orientation," so
that they will consider all three alternatives when faced with an
intervention decision.

Skill in Personal Counseling and Individual Consultation. In
every training program there is need at various times for individual counseling with trainees who are feeling lost or frustrated in the training activities or are experiencing problems of
motivation or commitment. Trainers need to develop skills in
identifying such individual counseling needs and in conducting
personal counseling that is supportive and facilitates personal problem solving without creating overdependency. Often a trainee needs
just a few minutes of special staff help to confront and clarify some
individual learning issue or some problem of bringing about connections between present learning experiences and on-the-job
responsibilities.

*Skill in Involving Learners in Planning and Evaluating Their
Learning Experiences.* Many trainers are threatened by expres-
sions of resistance, rejection, and frustration on the part of
trainees. It is crucial that future trainers develop competence in
encouraging learners to provide feedback about their reactions
to their learning experiences. Future trainers must also learn how
to help learners develop the criteria and skills for evaluation of
their progress in the training program, and how to involve learners
in the collaborative planning of the training design as it develops.
There is no greater motivation for learning on the part of volunteers than the opportunity to influence the decisions of their
trainers in developing and modifying their designs for learning.

*Competence in Documenting and Evaluating Training Pro-
grams.* The failure of most trainers to accumulate and share
their learnings about training is most unfortunate. Few training
experiences are documented for future use or for sharing with
trainer colleagues. Most trainers have little skill or experience in
developing and using evaluation techniques as a means for guid-
ing the improvement of their own practices and for validating

those that should be shared with others. Also, very few trainers know how and where to seek out the documentation that does exist. Included in such documentation should be an assessment of what worked and what didn't work in meeting training objectives. It is crucial that a body of knowledge about effective training procedures and designs be accumulated as a pool of resources for the thousands of trainers who need materials to help them enrich their training designs and skills.

Skill in Using and Developing Training Materials. In the first edition of this volume the authors, in the Epilogue, suggested the development and sharing of multimedia resource materials—tapes, filmstrips, charts, video tapes, etc. to enrich resources for the training of volunteers. In 1974 the authors completed such a training resource package specifically for use as a supplement to this book.[4] The taped episodes in that package are related to the different chapters of this volume—future trends, motivation, recruitment, training, rewarding and administering. There is a critical need to develop a stockpile of more specific training materials, such as case examples, taped episodes, filmed confrontations, 5- or 10-minute "theory sessions," and briefing sheets for skill-practice exercises. In every training activity there is some opportunity to develop, at least as a by-product, training materials which would make a significant contribution to this stockpile. Skill in the development of materials should be learned by all trainees.

Competence in Developing Teamwork Skills. Most training activities are conducted by teams of two or more trainers. In some cases a senior trainer helps develop additional trainers by working with one or two experienced interns. The development and use of skills of collaboration has high priority as an objective in programs of training trainers.

Professional Development Designs and Activities for the Training of Trainers

The Intern Team with Senior Trainer. One of the most effective ways to develop trainership skills is to design and conduct a variety of training events for an intern team under the leadership of a senior trainer. The intern trainers have the opportunity to learn from the modeling of the senior trainer and from observing

[4]DEVELOPING YOUR VOLUNTEER COMMUNITY, NTL Learning Resources Corp., Fairfax, Va., 1974.

and discussing one another's activities. This type of trainership design also provides much needed practice in team development skills and problems of colleagueship, because there are many forces working toward competition between the interns and dependency and counterdependency in relations with the senior trainer. Careful and creative handling of the relationships with the client population is a must. In such internship training designs it is critical that there be plenty of opportunity for the interns to be observed, to participate in feedback discussion, and to collaborate in designing a variety of training activities to prevent their having only a limited experience with one type of design and training activity.

Co-Trainer Apprenticeship. Apprenticeship with a senior trainer is another pattern for learning trainership skills through observing, planning, and evaluating with a senior trainer as model and supporter. One of the problems with this design, as with the intern design described above, is that there are strong forces operating against risk taking and experimentation because the training is in a context of "playing for keeps." Because of this problem, some of the other designs mentioned below are important supplements to learning trainership through fieldwork.

Simulation and Role-Playing Practice Opportunities. One of the most effective ways to provide reality practice is through role playing. The trainees jot down on cards the types of client reactions and intervention problems they find it most difficult to cope with. These cards are put in a pile in the middle of the table, and a card is drawn. Two trainees leave the room, including the one who put the card in. The rest of the group create role-playing episodes involving the critical issue or event. The two trainees are brought back, and one takes the trainer role in these episodes while the other sits behind listening and thinking about all the alternatives one might use if one were the trainer. After a brief practice period of perhaps ten minutes, a signal is given and the second learner takes the trainer's seat. The first learner watches, noting differences in their approach and again thinking in terms of other possible alternatives. There is then a "stop session" while the real trainer leads a discussion about the intervention decisions that have been observed, getting the reactions of the group and comparing the interventions of the two "trainers." The trainer helps review the alternative possibilities and generally supports the development of a flexible repertoire of intervention decisions and skills. This pattern of practice continues with other members of the group moving into the practice roles.

One important value of this kind of training activity is that all members have a chance to identify with and to learn the roles of different types of trainees, getting insights which help them as they move into the role of trainer. The fact that all of the learners have a chance to observe and criticize and support each other greatly multiplies the resources available for learning on the part of each one.

A similar opportunity to learn the skills of designing is provided by giving the learners a data sheet about a particular client population and its level and state of expressed need for training and asking them, in groups of three or four, to create appropriate training designs. These are reviewed, criticized, and revised. The same cycle is repeated many times with a variety of trainee populations and situations to be planned for. Unfortunately, this practicing of design skills is neglected in most of the learning programs for trainers.

Rotation of Trainership Role. Another favorite type of trainership opportunity has been called the "pass the ashtray" technique. In this design the trainees operate together as a training group. Whoever has the ashtray at a given moment is designated as the group trainer, while the trainer of trainers sits as an observer and diagnostician. Anyone can ask for the ashtray and take over the role of trainer, or the trainer can pass the ashtray to any other member at any time, but must do so by the end of a given time period, usually about 15 minutes. After two or three group members have had their trainership practice, the senior trainer holds a clinic session, sharing the observations of their performance and getting the group involved in reviewing, discussing, and analyzing the trainership skills they have witnessed in the practice session. Many variations on this procedure are possible. One that is frequently used is to have co-trainers practice together so that additional aspects of teamwork and collaboration can be reviewed as part of the learning about trainership. Sometimes the senior trainer is asked to sit in briefly as a trainer to demonstrate some point of intervention technique that has been brought up in the analysis.

Recording and Review Session. Still another widely used procedure is to tape record or video tape the practice session and to conduct analytic review sessions by viewing the video tape or listening to the audio tape. Such tape listening or viewing is a very time-consuming procedure, so usually it is necessary to select certain brief excerpts of tape to be used.

Use of Temporary Client Groups. It has proved quite feasible in many trainer-of-trainer programs to have a team of clients (e.g., children, teen-agers, adult volunteers) available on call when a practice opportunity is needed. These voluntary helpers function as a temporary client group and provide feedback. The opportunity to get direct feedback from clients in the context of practicing one's trainer skills, where the situation is defined clearly and openly as a practice opportunity, provides greater freedom to experiment and to risk trying new styles of behavior. We have found that children relish the opportunity to be helpers in the training of adults and do a very responsible job of providing feedback.

Trainership Institutes and Back-Home Practice. One of the most successful approaches being utilized by some professional groups in the training of trainers involves a two-part institute, often lasting three or four days. The trainees function first as learners, with the trainer-of-trainers taking the trainer role. Then, during the second phase, the trainees switch to the trainer role, practicing trainer skills with observation and consultation from their trainer. During this first institute they arrive at designs and commitments to try out during an interim period of perhaps a month, after which there is another institute. The focus at the second institute is on the exchange of trainership skills, consultation on designs, and opportunities for further practice. During the interim period it may be feasible to have an arrangement with the trainer so that telephone conferences can be conducted to review designs and to discuss training problems being met by the trainees in their back-home situations.

Discussion of Intervention Possibilities. Another favorite approach is for the trainers to describe briefly or to act out a critical moment where trainer intervention is needed. The trainees then jot down briefly all the possible interventions they can think of, select one or two which seem to them the most appropriate, and write a rationale for their choice. The trainees' decisions are then reported, and the trainer leads an active discussion of the comparative advantages and the value issues involved in the various intervention possibilities.

In summary, it is critically important to design a variety of practice opportunities that give trainees freedom to experiment with the trainership role, exposure to a wide repertoire of intervention models and practices, and the opportunity to design many types of training activities and to deal with a wide range of critical training problems and intervention issues.

An Illustrative Trainership Program

To provide a concrete example of an approach to some of the training-of-trainer activities discussed above, we shall describe one trainership program, a 2½-day institute for trainers from a number of community agencies. The flow of the institute is as follows:

Friday Noon. When they arrive at the motel at noon on Friday each trainee is handed a guide sheet. It asks them to stop briefly in a small room off the lobby and to play one of the three or four cassette tape recorders they will find there. As they listen on earphone attachments to the brief tape, they hear the trainer welcome them and clarify the objectives of the institute, which are also printed on the guide sheet.

The trainees have been asked to bring their own tape recorder with two or three blank cassettes. If they have forgotten this or do not have one, they are told to check one out on a rental basis from the motel desk. The orientation tape asks that, after getting settled, they dictate a reflective set of self-observations of their feeling about become a learner. They are asked to listen to the various voices they have within the self which are taking different postures about the energy and time and status issues involved in being at the institute and assuming the role of learner. They are also requested to dictate a fantasy observation of self functioning as a trainer six months in the future. The trainee is to describe concretely that client population being worked with, and what they see and hear themselves doing that makes them pleased with their progress as a trainer since the institute six months ago. The tape also tells the trainee where the buffet lunch can be secured when ready to go down, join co-trainees at one of the tables, and share any of the things put on the tape that feel o.k. to share. The briefing sheet announces lunch at 1:30 p.m.

Friday, 1:30 p.m. The 30 trainees have come in and have gathered at tables of six to eight, after picking up their buffet lunches at a side table. On each table are felt-tip pens and materials to make their name badges, and there is considerable interest on the part of the trainees as they see names going on and feel free to ask questions about each others' back-home situations. But the conversation soon changes to the material each worked on in his own room. They cautiously begin to share their expectations and hopes for the institute. The program notes invite them to have a leisurely lunch discussion and to convene for a general session at 3 p.m.

Friday, 3 p.m. The general session starts in the same room with the same table groups, after a ten-minute break to clear the tables of dishes. The first activity of the general session is for each person to fill out a brief process observation sheet on which they list some of the factors they think have been operating at their table to inhibit free and open communication and rate on a five-point scale how productive the conversation was, and how satisfied each feels with their role in it, with reasons. The table members then share their data. Each table is asked to make a brief report on its productivity and on the major restraints to openness which were identified. This process discussion period takes about a half hour. There are brief and interesting reports from most of the tables about their observations and evaluations.

Then the tables are provided with manila folders and string, and each participant is asked to write on one side of a folder name, location, type of trainership function, the type of client population worked with and agency connected with. The trainees hang these manila folders around their necks with the string and have a 10-minute "milling period" while background music is played. They look for others with whom they can create a work group that will provide the most possibilities for backhome collaboration and support, in view of location and types of functions.

In ten minutes these new groupings have been achieved, and the new table groups are ready to move ahead with the next phases of work. Their first job is to share their fantasies about their trainership development and their priorities for personal learning needs as they conceive them at this time.

Friday Evening Session (7:30-9:30 p.m.). The institute leader, using an overhead projector, presents some eight dimensions to be considered in creating training designs. Each dimension goes up on the overhead projector screen, and the light is left on after the presentation is completed.

Mimeographed case descriptions of three different macro-design tasks are then passed out to all tables. Each case description specifies a client population (e.g., a set of 20 married couples, a population of black and white teen-agers from the same high school, a group of black volunteers from a deprived area, etc.) and the length of time available for a training activity and gives some background data about training needs as they have been expressed. Each table group selects one of the three design tasks to work on and has an hour to develop a design for the training activity, using the institute staff as consultants when desired. Each table team is asked also to indicate the additional diagnostic data they would like to have about the client population and to call on any one of the staff members to respond with the information, if it would reasonably be available. When they have completed their tentative designs, adjacent table groups present their designs to each other for suggestions and criticisms. Staff are involved in each session. After a half hour of review and criticism the design teams have an opportunity to use another half hour in redesigning their training activity. These new designs are recorded on a ditto master by one of the table members, so that all designs can be run off immediately and be available as a resource for everyone at the conference.

As soon as its design is complete, each table team conducts a review session for itself on two topics: "What questions would we like to pursue with the staff leadership on the principles and techniques of designing training programs?" and "What have we learned about the problems and the techniques of team development from our experience in working together as a trainer team?"

Saturday, 9 a.m.—Review of Learning and Questions About Designing Training. In a general discussion session the staff respond to the tables' questions and observations of the previous evening concerning the principles of design.

Saturday, 10:30 a.m.-12 Noon—Development and Operation of Training Exercises. The staff present, in a brief conceptual input of 15 minutes, some of the major types of purposes for "micro-designs" or training sessions within a flow of total training designs (e.g., conceptual input sessions, skill practice sessions, interpersonal sensitivity). The trainees at each table then conduct a 10-minute brainstorm session on all the different purposes of training sessions that they can think of. These are recorded on sheets of newsprint, which are then put on the wall as an exhibit of ideas from all the tables. A volunteer committee agrees to edit and integrate all the brainstorm sessions into a report to be ready after lunch.

During lunch the staff members identify the major types of microdesign tasks listed by the table groups.

Saturday, 1:30 p.m.—Microdesign Practice. The staff put up along the wall a series of newsprint sheets with headings of different types of design tasks (e.g., a design exercise on giving and receiving help, a conceptual presentation on resistance to change, a practice session on preparing to apply one's learning back home). The trainees sign up to work as design teams on the tasks of their choice, and for the next hour they work together creating session designs. The staff circulate offering consultation to the teams as needed.

Saturday, 7:30-9:30 p.m.—Design Fair and Consultation. Each team has its "booth," manned at all times by at least one member of the team. Everyone moves around and studies the training design creations of the other design teams.

Sunday, 9-11 a.m.—Intervention Practice. This period of two hours is set aside for each table group to practice process intervention decisions and actions. The staff help each group organize its practice opportunities so that all members can practice trainer skills and consultation skills and have their interventions discussed and reacted to. A second round of practice activity follows, in which each table group operates as a task group planning for work with a back-home client system. The group members are given the responsibility for acting as consultants on group process or group efficiency and for making process interventions that would help the group in its task work. There is a very active general discussion session about the differences observed between the earlier group activities and trainership, focused on learning process skills, and the "task group" activities focused on the performance of some task, in which process interventions were aimed at improving the productivity of the task work.

Sunday, 11 a.m.-12 Noon, 1:30-2:30 p.m.—Resource Demonstration Fair. In the final workshop activity the trainees divide up into trios to explore and demonstrate the use in training activities of various types of resource materials, including large newsprint, record players, tape recorders, overhead projectors, art materials, film clips, filmstrips, etc. Each team has the responsibility for demonstrating various training innovations to their peers in the multiple-booth fair.

Sunday, 2:30-4 p.m.—Final Session. In the final session of the institute each table focuses on exploring the feeling of each of its members about the need for further trainer development opportunities and help. The members identify ways of being helpful as resource persons for each other in their development as trainers back home on the job. They also discuss their needs for periodic help from senior trainers. Specific plans for next steps of development and report are reviewed with the staff.

This illustration is just an illustration! There is no implication that one weekend is enough for a trainer-of-trainers program. For example, such a weekend might be the start-up of a program of three institutes, six weeks apart. There might be need for more orientation to the specialized content of particular volunteer training programs. But the illustration does focus on ways of teaching some of the major ingredients of training competence summarized earlier in this chapter. The training for each of these competencies provides a guideline for the development of the expanded and continuing trainer-of-trainers program.

VIII Administration of Volunteer Programs

Administration of volunteer programs and the role of the administrator has changed very much in the last few years. As volunteer programs grow and become a more important part of ongoing services to people, the job of the administrator as well as the scope of the programs will continue to change. Before we take a look at the changing role of the administrator and the kinds of characteristics a good volunteer administration has, let us focus on the persons who are volunteers today and who are available to us as resource persons to deliver more humane and individualized human services.

Who are the volunteers today?

This question could be answered in a variety of ways. Let us take three avenues of approach to answering it. One might be according to the groups, organizations, agencies depending on volunteers to extend their services. These might be divided as follows:

1. Public agencies, that is, governmental tax-based organizations such as public school systems, public welfare systems, community mental health agencies, community hospitals, correctional agencies, public health facilities, cultural facilities, recreational systems, and others.

2. Privately financed agencies and/or organizations such as the YMCA, YWCA, Girl Scouts, Boy Scouts, Campfire Girls, Girls Clubs of America, Boys Clubs of America, Family Service agencies, Voluntary Action Centers, community centers and settlements, and many others. We could also include the private business sector—particularly those businesses and industries encouraging their personnel to get involved in volunteer efforts in the community. This is an important and an increasing source for volunteers and support of volunteer programs.

3. Cause efforts, including grass roots action-orientated cause organizations such as student protest groups, neighborhood and community improvement groups, self help groups, legal counseling groups, child and family advocacy groups, draft counselling groups,

and other local and national action groups which may be either temporary or permanent. Characteristics of these groups are that the persons involved in them have a commitment to a particular cause and often special abilities and resources to help in the forwarding of that cause. Many of the new cause organizations are more informal in their procedures and able to change as they need to.

Volunteers in all these three groups work in a variety of ways and take on different roles depending on their abilities and interests. They may be on policy and decision making bodies such as boards of directors, or they may give direct service such as tutoring, or they may be involved in direct action implementing policies and decisions made by the decision makers. Some volunteers also see their roles as catalysts and change agents, either to help bring about change within the organization in which they serve, or they see the organization as the impetus for change in the community.

Another way to look at the volunteer world is to divide it by the functions of the community. In each of the functions there are volunteers serving together with professionals to extend services. These functional communities are described in more detail in Chapter X. They include:

1. the recreation and leisure time community (public and private recreation and leisure time efforts as well as commercial and business recreation).

2. the cultural community (both public and private cultural efforts including the arts, dance, music, writing, drama and museums).

3. the educational community (public, private and parochial schools, both formal and informal adult education).

4. the economic community, including private businesses.

5. the political community, including governmental functions as well as political organizations.

6. the welfare community (private and public welfare efforts and some union efforts in relation to the welfare of the workers).

7. the religious community including volunteer opportunities such as teaching Sunday School and the provision of a variety of programs and educational activities for younger and older people in church settings.

8. the health community including both physical and mental health programs, financed by public, private and business sources.

9. the public safety community, including probation, parole, the court, the police and other correctional efforts and activities.

10. the mass communication community including TV,

newspapers, radio and other kinds of mass communication on both small and large levels.

11. the physical, geographic or ecologic community including opportunities for volunteers to serve as planning aides, newcomer welcomers, statistical documenters, researchers, etc.

A third way to classify the volunteer world is to divide it into two categories of volunteer person power, including the underutilized, the potential volunteer, and the more utilized, more fully tapped volunteer. There is great variation as far as the utilization of some of these people is concerned. We seem to be moving from, for example, not tapping elders to a great emphasis on tapping the senior volunteer, so that some of these categories are certainly in an era of transition. However they still include as follows—

- *The nonjoiners or unaffiliated persons.* Most recruitment efforts are aimed at people who already belong to something such as a known organization or church, and therefore can be motivated through that organization. Traditionally very little has been done to recruit, select and place the person who is not already in an organizational group.
- *Men, especially single men.* The middle aged, married white business man may be found on many boards, but generally there are fewer men than women working as volunteers. Yet, the primary need of many organizations is for male volunteers.
- *Minority group members.* People of all races, ethnic groups, and religious groups depending on the community, may find themselves in minority groups which are largely ignored in the recruitment of volunteers. These may include Buddhists, Moslems, Native Americans, Blacks, Mexican-Americans, Orientals, and many others whom we haven't thought to tap.
- *Persons lacking formal education.* The person who has not had at least a high school education is often looked down upon by the professional recruiter. As yet, many of the application blanks for volunteer workers ask that the volunteer indicate the level of education. However, it has been found that formal education has very little to do with the ability and commitment of volunteers.
- *Persons in rural areas.* Agricultural extension agents and other professional workers tell us that it is difficult to recruit rural people who may live far from one another, but here is a most likely source if transportation problems can be worked out.
- *The Young.* Though recently encouraged to tutor, to work in hospitals, and to work with the elderly, the young still find volun-

teer opportunities difficult to come by.

- *Physically and mentally handicapped persons* are often not sought as volunteers. This is beginning to change due to some of the self help movements, where for example a former drug user becomes a volunteer counselor to a present drug user, and someone who's been through a cancer operation counsels with persons about to have such surgery.
- *Institutionalized persons,* whether they be in prisons, forestry camps, mental hospitals, foster homes, or other institutions have rarely been recruited as volunteers.
- *Blue collar workers* in some areas have not been recruited at all.
- *Labor Union members* have also been underutilized so far, though in some parts of the country labor unions are beginning to be tapped for their expertise and to help recruit their members as volunteers.
- *Elders.* The older segment of our population has been overlooked as potential volunteers until very recently. It is true that in some parts of the country there is a shift of emphasis to recruiting seniors as volunteers and they are found to be both available and able.

Clusters of more highly utilized volunteers include—

- Middle-aged, white, married women.
- Middle-aged, white, middle and upper-middle class business and professional men.
- Persons with religious affiliations and motivations.
- Educated, high status minority men and women.
- Visible, experienced volunteers, that is, volunteers who are so active that everybody in the community knows and wants them, even if in name only.
- Members of certain organizations and social groups.

Having looked at who the volunteers are today, let us now turn to the changing role of the volunteer administrator.

The Changing Role of the Volunteer Administrator

It is clear that a new profession is emerging in the volunteer world. It is the role of the volunteer administrator, director, coordinator, who oversees and supervises a volunteer program. We can see this emergence not only because so many more paid volunteer director opportunities are available, but also because community colleges and universities are beginning to offer courses and degrees in the field of volunteer administration. The volunteer administrator may be the executive director of an agency or organization utilizing a large number of volunteers in order to carry out its services. Or the volunteer director may be a middle management person within an organization in charge of the volunteer program. Some examples of the latter would include volunteer directors or coordinators who manage school volunteer programs, volunteers in probation programs, docent programs in museums and zoos, hospitals, mental health centers and business organizations where they are often known either as director of volunteers or director of community relations, and in many other settings. Most directors of volunteer jobs are full-time paid positions, but some are as yet part time or staffed by a volunteer who does not get paid for his or her services.

One of the more recent developments in this field is the emergence of volunteer coordinators in over 20 states in the United States at the state level directly responsible to the governor of that state. These administrators are usually responsible for initiating or continuing volunteer programs in state financed and run departments and institutions. This is a powerful, able group of professional men and women who are making great impacts in their states in recruiting volunteers to serve in state services.

Many cities also have hired volunteer coordinators or directors who are directly responsible to the Mayor or governing officer of that city. Here the volunteer administrator is responsible for helping initiate volunteer programs in city departments and services, including such departments as city planning, the library, recreation services, police services, tourist bureaus, and others.

The volunteer administrators in all of these situations and roles find, besides *new courses* at institutions of higher learning, other *new supports available*. These include the many new professional organizations that have sprung up to organize and support persons administrating volunteer programs. These include the directors of volunteers and agencies in many cities, the American Association of Volunteer Service Coordinators, the volunteer coordinators in hospitals, the school volunteer movement and associations, volunteer coordinators in parole and probation, and others. Many of these organizations have national officers and headquarters with regular national and regional meetings. Others are more localized, but the common purpose is to provide educational and support opportunities, as well as up to date information to the members.

Yet another support organization is the National Center for Voluntary Action, which has related services including a national clearinghouse where information on a vast variety of activities in the volunteer world is readily available, and a regular news sheet which gives information on current activities, work shops, people, books in the field. There is also the Association of Volunteer Bureaus available for persons working in such bureaus throughout the country. Other national supportive agencies and organizations are listed in the bibliography of this book.

It is clear that the *role of the volunteer administrator* is more than just administration. It is indeed a new multi-faceted, challenging and versatile role. It includes the following kinds of "hats": the administrative hat, the public relations or community relations hat, consultant hat both within the organization and to organizations in the community, and a training hat, which includes the training of relevant and appropriate staff and volunteers. The latter functions require for most people additional educational help and support to learn consulting and training skills.

New Confrontations and Opportunities

Certainly the massive changes going on in the world, in our country, and in the volunteer world bring with them new opportunities as well as new confrontations. These include more *demanding volunteers*, that is, volunteers who are more conscious of their rights, their wishes, the way their services are utilized, and who in many cases demand good training, good placement, and a contract that spells out what they expect of the agency and what the agency expects from them. New human service teams are developing also. These include interdisciplinary teams of which volunteers may be one or two members, for example, the principal, teacher, paid instructional aide and volunteer; or the doctor, nurse, social worker and volunteer in a hospital. Another kind of team that is developing is the team which may not be interdisciplinary but one in which each person brings very different resources. This is the team that includes a professional, a paid paraprofessional, and a volunteer. The implications of this development are that the administrator needs to be able to help human service teams become formed, maintained and trained.

The *women's movement* has surfaced many concerns about the second class citizenship roles they feel women take when they become volunteers. Their criticism has been mainly aimed at the service volunteer, because they do believe that volunteers are needed to help cause social change to happen. Their criticisms have certainly been direct and in many cases are helping organizations and agencies to evaluate whether they are giving the best kind of opportunity to the volunteer to serve in meaningful ways, both to the volunteer and to the agency. Also the women's movement, and particularly the National Organization for Women, is concerned about good contracts for volunteers that include adequate insurance coverage. The volunteer administrator obviously needs to learn how to handle these confrontations and criticisms and be able to interpret clearly what volunteers are doing and how both the needs of the volunteer and the needs of the clients of the agencies are being met through volunteer services.

A number of *unions* are also concerned about the increasing size of the volunteer movement. Their concern largely centers around the fact that they want to be sure that all the possible persons eligible to be employed are employed. Their criticism of volunteer programs is mainly aimed at making sure that volunteers do not replace paid employees or are placed in positions where paid persons belong, and that volunteers are not used an as excuse to cut budgets, particularly personnel budgets, in any way. Most persons in the volunteer world would heartily agree that volunteers not be recruited to replace paid personnel but rather to extend professional services to clients.

There is a *raised consciousness about budgets* that confronts the administrator. This has to do both with fewer funds being available in many places, as well as the better utilization of the funds that are granted. Evaluation and accountability are important aspects of good human service administrations, and volunteer administrators need to know or to learn how to make and defend realistic budgets. Further than that, they are now often required to know how to frame and write proposals for funds that may be available for their program, and to be able to evaluate these programs.

Ambivalent top administrators may be another source of confrontation. There are many administrators who know that a volunteer program will help extend their services. However, some are really not convinced of the wisdom of having volunteers as part of their agency operations. Many of these administrators need to be included in the planning and decision-making of the volunteer program so that they can be more knowledgeable about it.

New educational and *renewal opportunities* are much more available and will certainly be helpful to volunteer directors, coordinators, and administrators in meeting some of these confrontations, and encourage them to enjoy the opportunity and challenge of handling these challenges in more flexible and comfortable ways.

The Volunteer Program as Part of the Total Organization

Often in the past the volunteer program has been seen as a rather low status part of the total agency organization. Often the volunteer coordinator was seen as a weak link in the chain or as heading a department into which could be pushed all those things and services that you didn't know where else to put. However, this is changing rapidly with volunteer programs and departments taking on new and added importance as their value as a part of humane human service organizations are being proven out. Also, the professional training of the directors makes them more able to be visible, effective, initiative-taking and heard in their organizations. Volunteer departments are rising in status and becoming more pervasive in their activities throughout most organizations. This changes the relationship of the administrator to the top executive as well as to those staff persons employed within the organization. Also this means additional relationships to peer management persons within the organization. Administrators may also relate to boards and/or advisory committees of the total organization, as well as to the specific group that helps formulate policy for the volunteer program.

Some characteristics of good volunteer administrative practices include the following:

1. *Clear, communicated, constantly evaluated goals.* It is important for volunteer programs to develop "do-able", understood, broadly decided upon goals. As the program matures, goals are often redefined, refined, and changed.

2. *Involvement of a "vertical slice" of persons in planning, problem solving and decision making.* It is imperative to include persons to be affected by planning, problem solving and decision making in the processes.

3. *The actual administration of the program benefits by involving volunteers and staff on an ongoing basis.* It seems self-evident that systems, in which many volunteers work, should practice what they preach. However, many volunteer systems do not yet encourage volunteers as teammates with paid staff. Together, they can keep an office open, get materials out, train newcomers, solve problems, and consult. It is the unique resources of the volunteers and staff combined that make for the richness of the program.

4. *Regular feedback and staff-volunteer meetings.* Planning,

evaluating, replanning takes place best when people have a regular chance to get together. As they do so, trust and open communication tend to get built.

5. *Short and long term spaces and places for volunteers* must be included in modern volunteer programs. Mobility and temporariness are an integral part of our society. Therefore, our programs need to have shorter and longer term volunteer jobs available, so that persons who cannot commit themselves for long periods will not be lost as a human resource for the program.

6. *Opportunities for orientation, training, and competence improvement and growth* are essential for both volunteer and staff. Persons serve for many reasons. Motivations vary widely from a need to become more competent and successful. It is, therefore, important to offer developmental opportunities before and on the job. Often experienced volunteers as well as staff members can be the leaders of such activities.

7. *Flexible ground rules are needed.* Modern organizations tend to write their rules as they need them. They also keep them to a minimum. They should not be cast in concrete; it may be necessary to change them in this fast changing world.

8. *Keep connection with similar programs*, so that practices can be exchanged; perspective rather than provincialism is encouraged; and strength is gained through joint efforts.

9. *Collaboration* with other agencies, organizations, and causes in the community is essential for a health program. To the extent the program is connected to and intertwined with the larger community, more and more human and material resources become known and available to be tapped.

10. *Recognition* of the importance of *all* contributors to the program at various times makes a program more humane. This may include regular recognition events, but even more important are the "we missed you yesterday", "that is a great idea, thank you", and "it's great to see you today!" At the elbow training (available where and when needed), individual conferences, and volunteer-staff meetings are also ways to recognize persons' contributions and importance.

Voluntarism Goes Interagency, Community-Wide, State-Wide, and World-Wide

Another important change to notice in this time of transition is that there are now many communities in which there is much collaboration between agencies around volunteer activities. This collaboration may include community-wide board training for new board members, or it may be that one agency recruits and refers volunteers for all of the organizations and agencies needing such volunteers. Other collaboration may be around development of community wide activity calendars and directories, community information and referral services, and community wide training activities for volunteers of many agencies. Certainly the community wide workshop which is planned by a collaborative group of organizations and looks at better recruitment and utilization of volunteers is a common occurrence in the United States these days. (see Chapter 9)

We have alluded earlier in this chapter to some of the exciting statewide and city activities. Often the state people will be helpful in making local collaborative activities a reality. They may offer technical as well as financial support.

The first *International Conference* on volunteerism was held in the United States in October of 1971. An organization known as the International Association of Volunteer Education, is in touch with volunteers and volunteer movements across the world. Many of its members have traveled to countries and cities abroad to learn volunteer programs that are developed or/and emerging there. Also there have been conferences both in the Philippines and in France in which a variety of international countries and groups participated. In 1974 at the 18th International Conference on Social Welfare in Nairobi, Kenya, another international group was convened to talk about volunteer developments, and as part of the Bicentennial there will be an International Conference of Volunteers in 1976. It can be said that voluntarism and volunteering has gone international. This may mean both new relationships and opportunities for both volunteers and volunteer administrators.

This is probably the most exciting time in the history of the United States to be active in the volunteer world. These times offer a tremendous opportunity for volunteers to make important contributions to the quality of life and the human services in their communities. It is clear that the volunteer administrator is a key person in translating the motivation, interest, resources and skills of volunteers into human, extension services to the clients of our people helping agencies and organizations.

IX Toward Improving the Quality of Community Life: Community-Wide Planning, Inter-Agency Collaboration, and Volunteer Participation Development

There is much criticism and puzzlement, by community leaders and citizens, about the lack of vitality and attractiveness of our communities and cities—the wasteful overlapping services, the fragmentation of professional effort, the overloading of a small core of leaders, the non-involvement of the majority, and a lack of clear direction and planning for growth and development.

In our work on voluntarism, and our concern for the vitality and development of democracy, we have become much involved in these overall problems of community life which are so important for all of us, and are a crucial focus for voluntarism.

The clearest path to the development of meaningful, rational goals, and the mobilization of community energy is the focusing of community-wide attention and deliberation on images of desired changes in the quality of life, on the process of making decisions about priorities for action, on the mobilizing of collaboration between organizations, agencies and institutions of the community, and on the involving of volunteer interest, wisdom, skills, time, and energy from all sectors of the community.

We have had exciting opportunities to work with some fifty communities of all sizes and complexities during the past five years, trying to discover ways of stimulating and facilitating processes of goal setting, collaboration development and citizen mobilization. We have become convinced that voluntarism, democracy, and the American community are ready for significant break-throughs to new levels of problem-solving, vitality, and support for a more satisfying way of life for all of us.

The illustrative case example which we are presenting below is an integrated description drawn from our sample of communities, as we have worked with them on refining the approach to "turning on communities" and developing the teamwork of volunteers, paraprofessionals and professionals from all of the private, public and business sectors of the city.

An Illustrative Case Example

In the condensed narrative sequence below we have described the highlights of a typical flow of community development activities as it has been clarified and tested by us in a variety of communities. At the end of the case we will comment on a variety of variations on this pattern in different types of community situations.

1. *The Startup Conversation*

Typically it starts with a telephone call or a letter from some community group (e.g., the Junior League, Chamber of Commerce, Community College, Business Council, City Planning Dept., Voluntary Action Center) which has a concern about the quality of community life and planning, the desire to stimulate collaboration, and a concern about some issue or issues such as the utilization of volunteers, improvement of education, coping with the lack of collaboration between agencies and organizations, or improving the process of long range planning. The first dialogue involves helping these initiators and explorers clarify the idea and possibilities of community representation and community involvement, thinking in terms of the sectors of communities which we have outlined in Chapter 8. This involves thinking through who might be added to the ad hoc planning committee, and who might be used as nominators to help identify the key leadership groups and individuals in the various sectors of community, representing racial, ethnic, religious, age, sex and income groupings, as well as representation from the different sectors. The committee is helped to carry out this nomination process to identify typically 100 to 250 key persons truly representative of all aspects of community life who will be invited to the community wide conference. Methods are available to make this an efficient and feasible process.

2. *The Invitation Process and Pre-Conference Involvement*

One great strength of this process is that no particular organization or institution is seen as the only visible sponsoring group. The sponsorship is a representative ad hoc planning committee which drafts the invitation letters indicating to the invitees that they are being invited because they have been nominated as key community leaders by a nomination process which has indicated that they are seen as key persons to participate in a community conference concerned with the quality of community life and the setting of community goals and the working out of creative patterns of collaboration between organizations to reduce budgetary waste, program overlap, unnecessary competition, etc. Everyone who receives an invitation is connected with someone on the planning committee who has handwritten a little note on the invitation urging a positive response. The invitation indicates the purpose of the conference, who is being invited, and what kind of outcomes are hoped for. It is made clear that participation in the conference needs to be a complete commitment for the one or two days because it is an integrated problem-solving process rather than discrete activities such as speeches which can be attended part time. In the case which we are presenting here, which is quite typical, the conference is a two-day event.

3. *Designing and Arranging for the Community Conference*

The planning committee divided itself into three teams. One team worked with consultants on the designing of the actual flow and materials for the conference. The second team worked on all the physical facilities, room arrangements, etc. for the conference. The third team followed through on the invitations and worked with the local newspaper, radio and other media on announcements about the conference, its purpose and the anticipated involvement of the total community in followup actions. This team also took responsibility for recruiting the squad of conference facilitators who would participate in a training session the night before the conference and work as members of the conference team during the event itself. Usually there is at least one facilitator for every table group of 8 people.

The committee located an excellent conference site in one of the old downtown churches which had a very good acoustically treated room large enough for 200 participants to work in table groups of seven or eight. They were able to supply flexible table arrangements from their large supply of card tables. A local newspaper contributed the supply of newsprint which would be needed during the conference; the school system contributed an overhead projector and portable loud speaker units, and several agencies contributed the needed name tags and other supplies. The church had the needed ditto machine and the committee planned to purchase the duplicating paper, ditto masters, felt tip pens, masking tape and other supplies from the conference fee of $15.00. A very modest buffet lunch was planned, and several organizations agreed to contribute "conference scholarships" if any of the invited participants felt the conference fee might be a hardship.

The Voluntary Action Center had agreed to have their telephone number used on the invitation letter and the subcommittee provided volunteers to cover the telephone at certain hours each day so that followup calls could be made to invitees who had not responded, and inquiries about the conference could be responded to by someone with good information.

The committee was planning on about 200 participants, so facilitators were needed for an estimated 25 tables of eight each. In order to do a thorough job of documenting the products of group thinking, as well as providing facilitative leadership, the committee decided to recruit two teams of volunteers for each table, a table documenter and a table facilitator. The committee found it remarkably easy to recruit fifty willing helpers from the Community College, the Junior Leage, the Junior Chamber of Commerce, and the staffs and boards of several local agencies. The image of a significant conference was developing through the grapevine, through the interviews and other brief stories reported by the local media. Because the conference consultants did not live in town, they arranged for several phone conferences with the subcommittee collaborating with them on the design of the conference. After the first telephone conference of an hour, the consultants prepared a tentative conference design and sent it to the members of the subcommittee to review so their reactions could be sent in and discussed at a second phone conference. The consultants suggested the purchase of a small plastic phone amplifier (about $15.00) so that the members of the committee could all talk together on the phone with the consultants utilizing just one telephone.

4. *The Day Before*

The day before the conference the consultants met in the afternoon, at the conference site, with the members of the "facilities team" to review the physical setup of the space for the small group work design, to pre-test the equipment, and to run off some ditto masters which they had brought with them for use in the evening training session with the facilitators and documenters. The plans for a rapid service buffet lunch, and for the continuous availability of coffee, tea, and soft drinks during the day were clarified. The chairperson of the local planning group reported with pride that he had been able to get a subsidy of $3,000 from a local foundation to support the production and printing of the conference proceedings and to subsidize some additional followup days of support from the consultants, if needed.

From four to six thirty that afternoon the consultants conducted a "micro-conference" with the fifty group facilitators and documenters and ten alternates to orient them to the steps and procedures of the conference, and gave them a chance to try out their own roles as table facilitators and conference documenters. High morale and much commitment to the significance of their own roles developed during this session.

The consultants then had dinner with the planning committee to go over last minute details and changes. The conversation was a mixture of anxious participation and preconference celebration.

5. *The Community Conference in Action*

a. *Getting Started*

As the conference participants arrived they found welcoming coffee, tea, soft drinks and coffee cake (baked by volunteers), a table with their name tag and a folder. One of the registration helpers explained that the number on the name tag indicated their table number, and then asked them to put their name at any and all appropriate places on the large chart on the wall. The chart superimposed on the rough map of the community, indicated the major sectors of community function (i.e., economic, political, religious, educational, recreational, cultural, etc.) and the briefing instructions asked participants to fill in their full name in the sector where they spent most of their time, and to jot in their initials in all other sectors where they were active in some way, either professionally or as a volunteer. They were then invited to find their table where their table facilitator would be waiting for them.

As soon as two people had arrived at a table, the facilitator and documenter began a conversation about the nature of their activities in the community sectors in which they had located themselves. The documenter kept notes on this information.

The conference had been announced for nine thirty. By nine forty-five, 80% of the 190 participants who had accepted the invitation had arrived.

The conference began with the chair person of the planning committee introducing the two conference consultants. They began things with a 10 minute interview with a panel of four well known leaders from the conference planning committee, discussing the origin of the conference and its purposes.

They then turned to a team of two members of the committee who had been summarizing the data from the lineup chart in the hall, in order to make a "who are we" report to start the conference. As they reported briefly the data on the number of participants related to each aspect of community functioning, one of the consultants wrote the data on the overhead projector transparency so that the total "who are we" report was visually up for everybody to see. One of the most interesting visible facts was the large numbers of persons who were active in three or more sectors of the community life in addition to their primary home base. The consultants pointed this out as a great "linkage resource" for the development of communication and collaboration between subparts of the community.

In three or four minutes the conference leaders gave a brief overall overview of the plans for the day, reminded the group that work would be terminated at four o'clock, and would be reconvened at nine thirty the next day to carry through until three thirty. The importance of continuous participation was again emphasized.

b. *Perspective on our Path*

By 10:15 participants were ready to launch into the first inquiry event of the day, which was a half hour exploration of significant highlights, events and trends in the history of the community which might help the understanding of the nature of the community today. One of the conference consultants stimulated an active dialogue between the head of the County Historical Society and a professor of history at the local Community College. They had both been asked to be prepared to share in an informal way interesting anecdotes and interpretations of major themes of community development, critical turning points and trends and insights that might help us all understand "why we are the way we are today" as a community. The table groups were then asked to hold brief discussions to formulate any further questions about community history and to offer comments about causes of "why we are the way we are today". The table discussions gave off a very active buzz and the question and discussion period was still going strong when it was terminated at eleven o'clock in order to move to the next phase of community diagnosis.

c. *What We Are Proud About and Sorry About Today*

Using the sensitivity to the past as a warmup and stimulus, the table groups were now asked to use the two pieces of newsprint on their tables to conduct two five minute brainstorms. They were asked to take the roles of observers of their own community, and in the first brainstorm to list as rapidly as possible all the things about the community and community life which they were proud of, and in the second brainstorm to list all the things about the community and community life which they were sorry about. Before beginning their brainstorms, the conference consultants put up on the overhead projector the four key rules of brainstorming and emphasized the importance of using these rules to insure productivity of the brainstorm activity. The table documenter acted as recorder for the brainstorms at each table. At the end of five minutes time was called to shift to the second brainstorm. At the end of the two brainstorms each table group was asked to spend a few minutes checking the two or three items with the "greatest prouds" and the "sorriest sorries". Each table group was invited to call out one of their priority items and by a show of hands, other groups indicated whether they had checked the same item. It was obvious there was quite an interesting consensus about what groups were proud about and sorry about in looking at their community. It was announced that the documenters would work as a committee to summarize these brainstorms as part of the conference report, and also during lunch hour they would be posted on one wall to be available to all the participants as a resource for reading and use during the rest of the conference.

d. *Images of Potential*

It was now 11:30 and the conference was ready for the third inquiry project, a trip into the future to develop the data needed for prioritizing community goals and exploring areas of consensus and dissensus. The conference consultants explained the nature of the trip into the future, proposing a one year time perspective, and explained that in going ahead one year and making observations of what was happening in community life and intergroup cooperation that pleased them with the progress in the community toward an improved quality of life. This was neither a fantasy trip nor a prediction trip, but rather a freeing up of an imagination to observe credible, realistic, usable images of potentiality which they could imagine could come to pass, given the right amount of collaboration and effort.[1] To start the trip the conference leaders asked for illustrations from anybody in the group that might be examples of what they would be seeing as they looked down one year from now and observed things that pleased them very much about the improvements of quality of community life. Two or three illustrations were quickly forthcoming from participations and it was possible to emphasize the importance of concreteness and of talking in the present tense about what they were actually observing from their position a year from today. It was then suggested that each of the participants take a minute or two to rev up their imaginations, jotting down ideas to prepare themselves for pooling their images at their table in order to arrive at a table report on images of life in their community a year hence. In a minute or two discussion began at each table, and the facilitators helped the members at their tables to clarify and articulate their images, and the documenter recorded them on a large newsprint sheet. By 12 o'clock each table had produced, tested and clarified a list of images of desired future which they were ready to post on the wall for a conference reading period.

The conference leaders announced that there would be a one and a half hour break for participants to pick up a buffet lunch to eat at their tables and for them to wander and read the future images reports and to check the four or five images which they personally felt were priorities. They were told that their checking would be the basis for generating the interest task forces to be formed in the afternoon, and that all participants would get their first choice of an interest group in which to go to work on plans for community action and improvement.

e. *Lunching, Reading, Checking*

The volunteer catering subcommittee, using the budget provided by the conference committee, had set up an active salad and dessert lunch on a long table in the hall outside the conference room so that participants could pick up their lunch easily and quickly, walking down either side of the table. Some participants began reading future images sheets on the wall and checking them before they ate, and others ate first and then began their reading project. At 1:30 there was a reminder that half an hour remained to finish the very important process of checking priorities, so that interest task groups could be established on the basis of the votes of the total 190 participants.

[1]Fox, Lippitt, Schindler-Rainman, *Toward a Humane Society: Images of Potentiality.* LRC Fairfax, Va. Chap. 4 & 5.

During this period the two conference consultants and three helpers from the planning committee were scanning the checks on the wall to see which items were definitely selected as interest group priorities. This involved combining items from different sheets which were very similar. By two o'clock it was quite clear that 12 or 13 images were very clearly frequently selected ones. Many others had two or three checks. The ones receiving the high priority ratings were:

  A Senior Citizen resource center
  A Community Talent resource bank
  A Coordinating council for child and youth development, advocacy and education
  A twenty-four hour "help for anybody for anything" service
  An interagency parent and family life enrichment program
  A Community leaders' exchange forum
  An Art Council (coordinating all art activities)
  A Teen employment and occupational exploration committee
  A Women's advisory and career development center
  A Community calendar planning group
  A Community "ombudsman"
  A Community closed circuit TV forum
  A low cost housing advisory group

This listing of interest groups was written on the overhead projector, with table location assignments. Before moving everybody into their first choice interest groups, conference leaders suggested that there might be some participants who felt that a very high priority had been neglected and one which they would like an opportunity to "sell" before people made their final choices. It was suggested that if any such new interest group could attract at least three or four volunteers, it could certainly form as one of the planning task forces. Two such additional groupings were formed on the basis of effective presentations by advocates. Everyone then stood up and moved to the table location of their chosen interest group. In two cases more than 12 people chose a particular group, so two interest groups were formed on the same topic to make it possible to have a more effective small group process.

  f. *Diagnosis and Action Plan Development*

During the next hour and a half each task force was helped by one of the trained table facilitators, to clarify and flush out in greater detail their statement of their image of a desirable outcome or goal image. They then did a diagnostic force field analysis of the kinds of resources and supports which would be helpful in movement toward this objective and the major barriers and blocks and inhibitors of such movement. From this process they identified the most important resources to be mobilized and the most important blocks to be coped with. They were then helped to brainstorm all the alternative possibilities for effective action and to use a planning sheet to formulate first steps of action and who would need to be involved in what ways to make these steps successful.

During this period each group was introduced to the procedure of a five to ten minute "stop session" in which they used a brief evaluation check sheet to look at their satisfaction with their own work process in their interest group and to share ideas about ways of improving their productivity as they continued to work. During this period of work the final plans and ideas for needed next steps were recorded on ditto masters so they could immediately be produced and made available for the participants in the other groups. The other thing each interest group did, in looking ahead for tomorrow, was to identify three or four persons either in the conference or not in attendence who might be important reactors to and testers of their ideas and plans. It was suggested that such persons might be either resource experts, or policy or budget gate keepers, or important sanctioners.

During this period the consultants were actively moving from group to group to support the facilitators and to help any group that was having difficulty in its planning process or in making decisions about those they wanted to invite for the review process the next day. Each group was responsible for doing its own inviting of the reaction panel members, either contacting them at another table to make an appointment for the morning, or to plan who would make telephone calls to invite key persons who were not present.

All participants received dittoed one-page summaries of the reports from the other task forces by the end of the afternoon.

g. *Pulse Taking and Preparation for Tomorrow*

As the participants left they jotted on a prepared feedback sheet their personal reactions about their own participation during the day, their evaluation of the progress and needs of their group, and their hopes for activity and support the next day.

The planning committee met to review the reactions and expressed desires for the next day, discussing needed changes in the design and checking out plans for Day 2.

Second Conference Day

A. *Feasibility Test Reviews*

The participants were remarkably on time the second day, with many evidences of vitality and eagerness to "get on with it". Coffee was picked up and taken to task force tables as members convened to move ahead on their planning. The conference consultants conducted a brief general session of about fifteen minutes presenting on the overhead projector a series of questions the group might want to consider using in testing the feasibility of their action ideas with the resource persons they had selected. There were about a dozen newcomers who had been recruited by telephone calls to come and help the particular task forces assess the feasibility of their ideas and their planning. These new participants were welcomed and given a brief perspective on what had happened the day before and on the importance of their particular function. They were invited to stay for the remainder of the conference, but it was also made very legitimate for them to give their input and leave during the course of the morning. Until 10:30 all of the task forces worked actively with their resource persons and with each other on critically testing their action strategies, their goals and their first-step ideas.

B. *Anticipatory Practice*

During the next hour the participants were introduced to the procedure of behavioral simulation or anticipatory skill practice. After a brief demonstration the facilitators helped each task force to identify critical confrontation situations they could anticipate in initiating their first steps of action, e.g., recruiting new key persons, responding to criticism and resistance, presenting a proposal to a key power group, being challenged by vested interest group. In each group there was an opportunity to "dry run" and try out such critical situations and brainstorm alternatives, strategies and actions for coping more successfully.

C. *Support for Risk Taking*

During the buffet lunch period the conference planning committee invited several of the key leadership figures of the community, particularly from the political and economic community, to comment on their feelings about the significance of the conference and of the planning activities of the task forces. They were invited to indicate not only their sanction and their support but their readiness to collaborate in concrete ways, e.g., providing meeting facilities, helping in search for needed money, linking to external resources such as county, state and federal resources.

Towards Transition and Continuity

The final period, starting about 1:30, was essentially a planning conference for each task force to clarify their division of labor for next steps, the time and place of the next meeting, their agenda for their next session, the interim work to be done by various members of the group, steps to be taken in recruiting any additional task force members, needs for continuing consultation, and the preparation of a two or three minute report to the total conference on their progress and their plans. At 3 o'clock the final general session was convened, and each task force made its public report, which was also documented by the conference documenters working with their particular task forces. The conference leadership made a commitment about the preparation and distribution of a conference report. They also welcomed and identified representatives of the media who had been invited in for the afternoon report session. They were encouraged to interview any of the task force group members after they had heard the several reports, in order to prepare any types of special interest stories they might want to report. A press conference had also been arranged with the conference leaders and several of the other key community figures to provide prospective and information on the total conference process and on the plans for continuity of effort.

A final personal evaluation form was filled out, which gave individuals an opportunity to evaluate the conference, to indicate their personal commitment, and to give guidance to the steering committee as to future needs for support and facilitation.

The conference planning committee had consulted with the elected convenors of each of the task forces and were able to announce a meeting in about a month of the planning committee with all of the task force convenors to assess progress and to clarify needs for future steps of action and coordination.

Observations on Variations and Results

The process described above has been remarkably potent in generating a continuity of successful community development activity. We would like to share with you some observations about the types of outcomes and also about the type of variations in this community action development design which have helped fit the design into the needs and structures of various communities.

One of the major variables is the time available for the actual conference. Often both time and money budgets are limited to a one day conference. If this happens, the second day activities described above become part of the followup action plans for each task force.

Sometimes the conference is held around a more specific and narrow theme such as community wide recruitment and training of volunteers, improving services for youth, new roles and opportunities for women, etc. In these cases the groups invited to participate are those appropriate to the particular topic. As a result new collaborative efforts and networks are often born.

Followup has been done in many of the communities that have participated in these collaborative community conferences. Here are some typical results of accomplishments.

- Task forces to coordinate volunteer activities have helped to establish new voluntary action and information centers.
- The need for collaborative action relating to some kind of 24 hour information and referral service has resulted in such services being set up.
- Directories of human services, often bi-lingual, have been prepared with regular up date plans as an integral part of this effort.
- Several student employment opportunity centers have been initiated.
- New, especially minority, leadership that emerged during the conference has become an important part of the community leadership structure.
- New facilities have been found or established for youth offenders.
- Coordinated community calendars have emerged, produced cooperatively by the Chamber of Commerce and the volunteer agencies.
- Courses on volunteer administration have been established at many community colleges and universities.
- Several community coordinating committees have been established with representation from the private and the public sectors.

Also there are some examples of continuity of efforts from the conferences. They take a variety of paths:
- Conference task forces who find a permanent "roof" or sponsor

(e.g., the task force on youth employment opportunities gets taken on by the mayor's commission on youth)

- Conference task forces who merge with an already established body to strengthen and often change the direction of that group (e.g., several task forces on development of low cost housing have merged with other groups working on this activity)
- Sometimes a task force does its initial work (e.g., exploring the establishment of a voluntary action center) and then the new board of that agency takes over. Often some members of the task force become board members.

Whatever the continuity the emphasis is that these efforts not be duplicators of already ongoing activities. Followup from these conferences must result in extension of already extant activities, creation of new needed community structures, or/and strengthened support of collaborative efforts in the community with new people involved in these processes.

X Images of Potential: The Volunteer Community

At this point we feel the need to pull together into some kind of conclusion our explorations into the various aspects of voluntarism—philosophy, recruitment, training, new roles, and interagency relations. A mere summary of what we have said would not be very exciting, either for you or for us. So we have decided to try to integrate our ideas and observations by taking a leap into the future. We shall observe in our imagination a community doing an outstanding job of identifying, mobilizing, and using its volunteer power potential.

To begin our search for this community of the future, we should clarify what we are looking for. What derivations do we make from our analysis in the previous nine chapters? Our ideal "Volunteer Community" would have as its goals the following:

1. To develop the necessary knowledge, skills, and resources to find, recruit, train, place, and support additional volunteers for service throughout the community

2. To increase the knowledge of men, women, and children in all parts of the community about the opportunities for volunteer service and to increase their motivation to offer their services

3. To extend greatly the range of places and ways in which volunteers can serve the community

4. To develop voluntarism in such critical and undeveloped areas of service as cross-age, cross-talent, cross-sex, cross-race, cross-social class, and cross-economic status

5. To experiment actively with the development of new human service teams of professionals, paraprofessionals, and volunteers

6. To develop new designs for the communitywide coordination of volunteer services

7. To increase the number of professionals who have competence as trainers of volunteers and as leaders of human service teams (This would include offering in the schools and colleges theoretical and experimental learning opportunities in recruiting, training, and leading volunteers and human service teams.)

8. To improve the linkage between federal and state programs and local leadership to assure use of all the relevant financial and program resources in the development of local volunteer services.

Keeping these goals in mind, let us leap ahead several years and see what a community that has been striving successfully toward them might look like. Let us take off in our helicopter and hover over our imaginary city, getting a perspective on all the types of activities that make it a vital and functional Volunteer Community: the activities of all those persons in the community who, as part of their daily life, and unpaid for their time and energy, are carrying out many of the necessary functions of a creative, developing, human need—meeting community.

The Volunteer Community in Action

The Volunteer Community we are observing can be divided into eleven subcommunities according to function: the leisure time and recreational community, the cultural community, the educational community, the economic community, the political community, the welfare community, the religious community, the health community, the public safety community, the mass communication community, and the geographic community. We shall observe each of these communities and see what kinds of volunteer activities are in progress there.

In the *recreation community,* volunteer workers function as referees, assistant recreation directors, "tot lot" supervisors, and teachers of crafts, games, hobbies, and dance. They are being used much more than previously as day camp and resident camp directors and counselors, and simply as resource volunteers who bring to the camp setting skills that the professional and para-professional staff may not have. Volunteers also act as youth leaders in youth agencies and church groups. They chaperone youngsters on trips and special events. Some volunteers are "on call" as resource persons for youth groups; they are available to offer transportation or to cook or to help with training in special skills. There is a whole directory of such talents that can be used when most needed. A Volunteer Resources Referral Service Bureau has been developed.

Elder-youth teams (made up of retirees and teen-agers) serve as discussion leaders for groups, as youth group advisers, and as visitors to shut-ins and handicapped youngsters and oldsters. Intergenerational teams of a "younger," a "middle," and an "older" have been formed to bring the three generational points of view to a group discussion series. Volunteers are also acting as connectors and extenders of agency services to community people of all ages, particularly those who are usually unreached.

In the *cultural community,* volunteers are being used extensively as tour leaders and other types of aides in the art, history, and science museums. Some are teaching courses in the museums. Others are acting as interpreters and guides at the zoo, helping children and adults to really enjoy their visit. Volunteers are leaders of community music, art, writing, dance, drama, and painting activities. They are often assistant class leaders or resource persons in classes taught by professionals. Volunteers organize and lead nature appreciation walks and talks. A pool of cultural resource volunteers is available to individuals and groups as leaders, experts, and helpers. These volunteers who are active in the cultural community are part of the Volunteer Resources Referral Service, so that they can be effectively identified and used. A few volunteers are acting as "cultural emissaries" in a variety of ways to poverty neighborhoods, to the elderly, and to the very young.

In the *education community,* volunteers are functioning as teachers' aides and school volunteers. The national school volunteer program is continually increasing in size and effectiveness. During school hours, adults, high school students, and junior high students are engaging in voluntary cross-age tutoring activities. Outside of school hours, there are many opportunities for tutoring both youngsters and adults who are in need of extra help to make their school experiences and life experiences more valuable and more fun. Special resource volunteers are available to schools, adult education classes, religious education activities, and the informal education activities that take place in the education community. Volunteer nursery school helpers, street crossers, playground aides, cafeteria aides, library aides, and administrative aides, as well as volunteer teachers on special subjects, are available from the Referral Service.

Volunteers are also making a very special contribution as curriculum idea helpers. Young and old have ideas of what makes a relevant, exciting, and challenging curriculum. Volunteers have been put on curriculum committees of schools and school districts in order to tap these ideas.

In addition, volunteers are being used extensively as counselors for vocational preparation, personal problems, and growth planning. These helpers represent a particularly valuable way to extend the schools' counseling services, which would otherwise be woefully inadequate. More individualized help to students through counseling has been very much needed, and the volunteers in our imaginary city's schools have been trained to extend this kind of service very effectively, with continuing training and supervision by professionals. The schools, in collaboration with the Family Life Development Council, are conducting a series of neighborhood parent institutes on the things parents can do to collaborate with the schools in the education of their children.

In the *economic community,* volunteers have been tapped as job developers and recruiters of the unemployed and untrained. They help young apprentices in many areas of work experience. They have made it possible to offer intern positions in a variety of occupations in business and industry to young people and adults who need this kind of opportunity. They also give the additional personal support that cannot be offered by busy supervisors. Retired businessmen are being used to counsel the young job seekers and to help the newly employed get started. The program of "outreach" to locate and involve the unemployed in training opportunities is manned by volunteers from the low-income areas of the community.

In the *political community,* volunteer vote getter-outers and poll helpers have been used for a long time. Volunteers are now beginning to help not only in campaigning, but also in governing the community. For example, hundreds of volunteers have been recruited to help think through a new urban planning scheme for the large city. Small group discussions have been set up with citizens who have been asked to give their opinions on what a good community would be like if they had a chance to help plan it. Volunteer aides to mayors, city councils, school superintendents, and others perform very helpful functions. It has been clearly demonstrated that volunteers can be trained in a disciplined fashion to become aides to a variety of political leaders who need more help than they can afford to pay for from public funds. Volunteers also act as connecting links, giving the political leaders closer ties to the community. A coordinator of volunteers has been appointed to recruit volunteers for all levels and areas of local government.

In the *welfare community* volunteers act as social work aides, visitors to the elderly, sick, and handicapped, housing finders for welfare clients, community helpers and informants, and waiting room volunteers. The latter make the waiting room experience a more comfortable one than it usually is, by helping clients find their way to the intake desk, taking care of their children if they are not part of the service sought, etc. Volunteers are being used to help find foster homes, to assist in adoptive parent interviews, to act as intake interviewers for agencies, to provide day care for children, to transport those who do not have transportation or are too handicapped to use it, and to connect welfare clients with the cultural, economic, educational, and health communities.

It is in the welfare community particularly that teamsmanship has been developed, because the professional, the paraprofessional, and the volunteer have very different resources to offer. Each has his own unique knowledge, connections, training, and sensitivity. Working together as a team, they are able to provide more extensive and higher quality services for patients, clients, and constituents.

In the *religious community* there have always been a variety of opportunities for volunteers, who have worked as religious education teachers, Sunday School transporters, camp directors and counselors, cultural activity leaders, board and committee members, and sometimes even volunteer guest lecturers on Sunday morning. In our illustrative community, opportunities have been increased and diversified. Volunteers are acting as interpreters to the foreign born who would like to attend a particular religious activity. Volunteers are taking leadership in presenting points of view for discussion, whether from the pulpit or in a more informal manner. Many new volunteers have been recruited. Particularly exciting are the use of volunteer pairs who have different social or racial backgrounds and the increasing use of teen-age couples and husband-wife pairs as volunteer teams. The interpersonal rewards of collaborative service add an important dimension to volunteering.

In the *health community,* which is increasingly taking responsibility for providing health services for all citizens, volunteers find their services constantly needed. They are working as neighborhood health center aides, receptionists' aides, medical social work aides, and visiting nurses' aides. Volunteers may also be viewed as health service extenders, who appraise citizens of the kinds of services available to them and personally connect them with the ones they need. Volunteers have long been used as fund raisers by the national medical research charities, such as the American Cancer Society. In our imaginary community, volunteers are also leading the fund raising for local community health needs that do not fit into the budget of the neighborhood health center, such as clothing for the newborn, certain kinds of medicine, and aids for the handicapped. They are serving as drivers for incapacitated patients and as crisis visitors to families who have undergone accident, illness, or death. (This is an adaptation of the Army's community service program of crisis visitors.) Many volunteers are working as consumer education aides and as consultants on diet and healthy living to people who need information and support.

The *public safety community* is just beginning to make use of volunteers. In the field of corrections, volunteers act as probation aides in a program known as Volunteers in Service to Offenders, as tutors in prison, as helpers to parolees. They deal with both juvenile delinquents and adult offenders. Volunteers are being trained to be court aides and counseling aides. Some are visitors to resident facilities, where they head discussion groups, help make renovations, or help prepare a resident in a correctional facility for his release and comeback to the larger society. Volunteers enable the local Halfway Houses to extend their services beyond the time and ability of the professional staff. Volunteers are serving as supportive "inviters" to persons who are trying to make their way back into society. Helping people to complain appropriately when they are being illegally victimized is another exciting challenge for a network of volunteers working with professional leadership and consultation. Growing teams of young former offenders are working with pre-teens and young teens as crime prevention aides.

When we look at the community's *mass communication services,* we see the beginning of some very new volunteer positions: as connectors to local newsworthy events and persons, as TV and radio station aides, and as volunteer announcers. Volunteers are serving as newspaper contributors, news alerters, and teachers helping the young to learn the skills of using the mass media.

A few volunteers are working as advertising aides, writing and selling ads of local significance. Volunteer fund raisers for the local educational television station make possible the airing of public information programs that could not otherwise be seen.

In the total *geographic community* one of the recent developments has been the concept of community neighborhood aides. These are volunteers who listen to neighborhood people's problems and perhaps help them solve them, or at least connect them to the proper source of help. Volunteer physical and social planners work with the professionals in these fields. Volunteers also serve as relocation aides, newcomer welcomers, visitor welcomers, and statistical documenters. The coordinating community is beginning to see that there is really no limit to the kind of help volunteers can give to other citizens in an organized fashion to make the community a more friendly and accessible one.

The examples cited above show only some of the ways in which volunteer work in this community of the future offers opportunities for people to serve themselves and each other. Through the use of volunteers, the community is able to extend *all* its services to all its citizens in a much more encompassing and usable way.

Mechanisms of Coordination and Training in the Volunteer Community

Several years ago a Coordinating Council for Volunteer Services was created in our Volunteer Community. It includes representatives from public and private agencies, the city government, the board of education, the community college, and the university extension service. One of the Coordinating Council's operating mechanisms is the Coordinating Committee on Recruitment and Referral, which uses a variety of techniques to discover potential volunteers and to recruit them for particular community needs. It keeps a computerized directory of information about their interests, skills, commitments, and experiences. The mass media collaborate very fully with this committee.

A second operating mechanism, the Interagency Committee on Training and Support, has developed a pool of trainers of volunteers and helps stimulate and coordinate a continuing program of training. Professionals on this committee come from the university extension, the community college, the American Hospital Association, the adult education department of the board of education, the training department of a local industry, the personnel department of the city government, and several local education and welfare systems. One active task force of this committee is the interagency team which is recruiting and training 100 pairs of volunteers to be leaders of parent education groups being formed and sponsored by many different agencies, organizations, and informal groups. Another very exciting task force focuses on cross-age helpers. This group attempts to support and stimulate a healthy growing-up process by recruiting older children, teen-agers, and retirees to help provide for the needs of infants, children, and youth.

Another operating mechanism activated by the Coordinating Council is the Committee on Service Innovations and Volunteer Recognition. Its purpose is to identify creative volunteers and significant human service innovations and to provide public recognition of outstanding volunteer service.

An interesting recent development is the formation of the Association for the Utilization of Volunteers. Any person, young or old, rendering any type of volunteer service in the community is eligible for membership. Dedicated to extending and improving the quality of voluntarism and promoting the appropriate use of volunteers, the Association promises to become a very influential group. It is working to improve the training of volunteers, to upgrade their service opportunities, to give them higher status, and to overcome professional resistance to their use.

Before we leave our illustrative community let's take a brief look at the variety of training activities going on there. The adult education department of the public school system has a leadership training course every three months for volunteers who are officers and chairpersons of local organizations and committees. The leadership of this training course is recruited by the Interagency Committee on Training and Support from the pool of well-qualified teachers in the various agencies. The community college has a very innovative and well-attended laboratory course for "people helpers," both paraprofessionals and volunteers. It provides skill practice and orientation to new ways to serve. The course developed by the American Hospital Association for its own directors of volunteers has been opened to directors of volunteers in all types of settings. The university extension service is offering several training opportunities, including an applied behavioral science course titled "Understanding Other People and Ourselves" and an advanced laboratory course for trainers of volunteers which focuses on the designing of training programs. Recently the extension service conducted a weekend work conference on cross-age helping which reviewed the most innovative and successful practices in this area of volunteer service.

The Coordinating Council for Volunteer Services conducts a two-hour luncheon workshop every other week where the focus is on sharing creative practices and helping the volunteers to support and stimulate each other in adapting and trying out new ideas. It is an open workshop for anyone to attend at any time. The Parent Education Task Force also has a continuing program for the leader pairs who have volunteered to learn how to conduct sessions with parents on "family life development."

This has been much too brief a glimpse of our Volunteer Community's vibrant programs for the development and use of all types of volunteers. But how did the Volunteer Community reach its present state? What initial steps can community leaders take to develop the vast untapped resources of volunteer service that exist in every community?

Action Strategies for Achieving the Volunteer Community

There are several effective ways to move toward a full mobilization of volunteer energy and commitment in the community. Here are four of the "start-up" strategies that were used in the development of the Volunteer Community we have been observing:

1. *Community Conference on Use of Volunteers.* A small interagency conference committee and a team of two training consultants designed a one-day invitational conference for all the key leaders of agencies, governmental departments, and organizations with programs using volunteers or having a need to develop volunteer resources. The 100 leaders met all day in a hotel ballroom, sitting at 10 round tables. During the first two hours they participated in a knowledge retrieval and utilization session in which the consultants briefly presented a series of research findings and generalizations about voluntarism, such as

the basic conditions for motivation and support of volunteers. Each table used a problem-solving design to derive implications for action from these principles, to diagnose factors inhibiting and supporting fuller recruiting and use of volunteers, and to develop strategies of action.

During a second period each table selected a case study of new uses of volunteers to work through in detail. One case dealt with the development of a telephone "hot line," in which volunteers are trained to answer callers' problem questions about health, welfare, and employment problems or refer them to other agencies, to counsel teen-agers about sex and drug problems, and to connect older citizens of the community with volunteer service opportunities.

Another case study was that of an "exchange of practice" session. Volunteers working with youth and adults on probation come together at a one-day meeting to discuss, retrieve, and document their successful practices. "Successful" being defined to mean those that have helped a probationer to live a more productive, healthy, and useful life.

In another case, the community has established a multipurpose center and developed an interagency coordinating board. This board consists of an intergenerational, interracial, intersex group of volunteers, professionals, and paraprofessionals. Many of the participants have never been on a decision-making body before. They have very different economic, religious, and educational backgrounds, and varied areas of experience. A small group of the board members and an outside consultant are planning the first training session for this new board.

In the fourth case study, people from many neighborhoods in the community have held a series of meetings about their desperate needs for child care centers as more and more of the mothers are going to work. With the help of a consultant from the state department of education, an articulate volunteer strategy planning committee is working to take a proposal for the studying and organizing of such centers to the state and then to the federal level of government.

A fifth case involved a professional consultant who lives in the Volunteer Community but does most of the consulting work elsewhere. The consultant is excited about the community's innovations and its utilization of all kinds of people as volunteers to provide social, cultural, recreational, health, welfare, and employment services. He/She is a "circuit rider," connecting the new ideas and practices of the community to the expressed needs of organizations and agencies in the neighboring communities.

Working on these cases gave the participants in the community conference an opportunity to experiment with the basic skills of documentation and interagency use of each other as resources. In the final phases of the conference, task forces worked on ways to organize a continuing program of effort on the utilization of volunteers. From these discussions the idea of the Coordinating Council for Volunteer Services emerged.

2. *Conference of Volunteers.* In a second start-up activity, an ad hoc sponsoring committee solicited nominations of innovative volunteers from all agency leaders. The nominees—men, women, teenagers, elders, suburbanites—convened for a lunch session and met until 5:30 p.m. They began with an "identification of interests" exercise, interviewing each other in pairs about their interests in volunteer activities. The data elicited were recorded on a manila folder suspended by a cord around each interviewee's neck. Then during a leisurely scanning period the participants wandered around reading each other's personal data and selecting two or three other participants with whom to meet and exchange ideas, skills, and experiences as volunteers. From this exciting conference the plan emerged for a Continuing Association of Volunteers.

3. *Interagency Training-of-Trainers Institute.* An ad hoc planning committee identified all of the professionals in the community with some responsibility for training volunteers. A questionnaire return indicated that 25 to 30 of them were ready to participate in a weekend institute for trainers, with a follow-up monthly seminar, led by two outside trainers with special skills in the area of volunteer training. The weekend focused on the skills of designing training activities and included intensive practice sessions on trainer skills.

4. *Local Survey of Volunteers and Volunteering.* A survey committee, working with a consultant from the university, designed a survey with three purposes: (a) to identify and describe briefly the programs and organizations using volunteers and to get basic data about each of the volunteers, (b) to locate needs for volunteers, and (c) to assess the available but noninvolved population of potential volunteers.

The team used a combination of questionnaires to agencies,

interviews with administrators and directors of volunteer services, and checklists for samples of the population in all walks of life. The findings of this survey were the basis for an invitational conference of agency and organizational leaders, as well as for stories carried in the newspapers and on local radio and television stations. The invitational conference established the need to form the Coordinating Committee on Recruitment and Referral.

Conclusion

We hope our illustration of a Volunteer Community of the future has provided you with a framework for summarizing our earlier chapters and for thinking about the exciting challenge of mobilizing and creatively utilizing the human resources of a community. Most of the elements of our image of potentiality can be found today in some community, but they have not been conceptualized and coordinated in any single community effort. The next steps are waiting to be taken. We hope we can help.

Epilogue

All of us read many ideas that stimulate us, but only rarely do we put them into practice. We hope the resources and methods suggested below will enable you to bridge the traditional gap between reading and implementing, between images and action, and will help you to adapt to your own situation any ideas you may have developed as a result of our presentation.

The resources for the development and support of vigorous and well designed programs of working with and through volunteers have expanded tremendously in the five years since we wrote the first edition of this volume. Particularly important has been the rapid development of the professional associations of Coordinators of Volunteers in many sectors of the volunteer community, e.g. the health sector, education, corrections, public service.

Also many more communities now have a Voluntary Action Center, or Volunteer Bureau, or some other local coordinating council to support the collaboration of all agencies and organizations which utilize volunteers. It is much easier today for you to find local colleagues to share and consult with.

It is also more possible for you to find, in your area, opportunities for professional training in the skills, strategies, and knowledges needed to develop and administer a volunteer program, or to develop the skills of designing and conducting training programs for volunteers. These opportunities may be found in a growing number of Community Colleges and Universities, and regional workshops sponsored by professional associations and Continuing Education Centers.

Perhaps it may be helpful to review some of the ways professional and volunteer leaders in voluntarism have found to guide and support their work.

Consultation Resources

There are a variety of ways of locating and using the help which makes so much difference in the quality and efficiency (i.e. reduction of mistakes) of your leadership efforts.

- You can telephone one or more consultants around the country to get help with a particular agenda of questions. If you want to be even more organized, send the consultants a list of the questions a few days beforehand. It is sometimes useful to talk with several consultants simultaneously, via special conference calls set up by your telephone operator.

- You can send a set of questions, either on paper or on tape, to one or more consultants, requesting that they tape record their responses and send the tapes back to you.

- If both your organization and your consultant have access to video tape and viewing equipment, you can tape the particular situations on which you need help and send the tapes to him. He then views them and either tape records or video tapes his responses. A telephone conference before you tape the situations is advisable, to ensure that you will include on your tape the things the consultant finds most useful.

- You can bring several consultants to your agency or organization for a diagnostic consultation day with all those who need help on a particular matter, such as designing a volunteer training program.

- You can arrange with outside consultants to visit on a periodic basis. For example, if your organization is designing a volunteer development strategy, you might call the consultants in initially to help develop the strategy, later to check how it is working out, and at some still later time to develop a continuing evaluation and feedback plan. You might then arrange for continuing visits on an annual basis.

Recognizing that leaders and organizations often find it hard to determine whom to consult regarding their needs, hopes, and plans for extending voluntarism we suggest you may want to check with one of the resource centers listed in this book.

Multimedia Resource Materials

This book has offered many suggestions for possible uses of such media as tape, video tape, recordings, and slides in volunteer recruitment, orientation, preservice and in-service training, and other areas. We hope that you will feel free to experiment with multimedia materials in all phases of your work. Multimedia packages of various kinds are now on the market. Two new resources, appearing in 1974, will be of especial help to administrators, consultants and trainers. They are: "Training Volunteer Leaders," a handbook to train volunteers and other leaders of program groups by the Research and Development Division, National Councils of YMCAs, New York, and "Developing Your Volunteer Community," a multimedia package developed by the authors with XICOM, Inc., New York. Available through NTL Learning Resources Corp., Fairfax, Va.

If your organization would like to develop its own multimedia materials, help is available from many universities and private organizations. As much as possible, any materials developed should be disseminated and exchanged with other organizations, to defray production costs and to "spread the wealth."

Short-Term Conferences and Meetings

Carefully designed meetings and conferences are one of the most important and effective methods of generating action. There are many designs to choose from, depending on the circumstances.

- One useful kind of meeting is the start-up problem-solving event, where problems are identified and possible ways to solve them are suggested. Such a meeting often gives rise to a series of planning and consultation meetings.
- Another kind of short-term meeting brings together representatives from different agencies to consider their common problems and to try to develop common strategies for coping with them.
- The "images of potentiality" meeting calls for participants to imagine themselves six months or a year hence and to write down what they see themselves doing in the organization and what progress they have made since the time of the meeting. The rest of the day is then spent working on ways to make the images a reality. This kind of meeting can be the foundation for an organization's long-range goal planning.

Short-term meetings and conferences, be they for problem census, policy making, goal setting, training, or inspiration, need careful planning to ensure that the desired results can be obtained within the time allotted. Consultants can be of great help in designing such meetings and conferences.

Continuing and Periodic Meetings

Regular meetings, especially for training purposes, can have a much more lasting effect than "one-shot" meetings after which the participants are expected to do everything right. People are more apt to implement what they learn when there is continuing reinforcement. Moreover, periodic meetings benefit the organization as well as the participants, by providing contact, support, and feedback.

To cite a model, two-day meetings for training change agents might be held every other month for a year. The work between meetings would be mutually agreed upon by the planners and the participants, with all meetings after the first based largely on the needs of the participants and on the ongoing work within their own projects.

A series of meetings can also be very fruitful in the training of trainers. Each session in the series might focus on a different way of helping people learn, such as large and small group meetings, simulations, role playing, and multimedia materials.

Staff meetings can be considered ongoing training and information meetings as well. Most staff meetings would benefit from being planned with more continuity. Perhaps a rotating committee of staff members could plan the meetings to serve the needs of all the staff, with "submeetings" for subunits.

Exchange of Practices

Every day volunteers and other social practitioners and people-helpers develop innovative, creative, experimental ways to help their clients. Usually, however, they have no way to document their new practices. They simply exchange them verbally and informally, and many get lost. It is estimated that thousands of inventive social practices are lost each year for want of a good way to get hold of them.

Our suggestion is that organizations using volunteers develop methods for bringing these social inventions to the light of day. One method might be to hold a cross-agency conference for volunteers in a particular field, such as those working with 16- to 21-year-olds. Using a little interview schedule, they can quiz each other about what they have found to be successful in working with this age group. A recorder or documenter can take down each respondent's name and address and his successful practice, so that it can be reproduced and used by others. Such a conference, incidentally, is also a good way to begin or strengthen collaboration between agencies, as it demonstrates their interdependence and enriches them both.

Continuing Exchange with the Authors

The authors deeply appreciate the flow of feedback and suggestions from readers, which have given significant guidance to this second edition. They invite continuing dialog, and can best be reached c/o Hilltop Seminars, 4267 San Rafael Avenue, Los Angeles, Calif., 90042.

TABLE OF CONTENTS FOR THE BIBLIOGRAPHY

Bibliography

I. Volunteers: Philosophical, Historical, and Evaluative Statements

Becker, Dorothy G. "Exit Lady Bountiful: The Volunteer and the Professional Social Worker." *Social Service Review* 38:57-72; March 1964. *Traces the history of friendly visiting, the volunteer precursor of social casework. Attempts to analyze which aspects of the original role are revelant today and which are not.*

Church, David M. *How To Succeed with Volunteers.* New York: National Public Relations Council of Health and Welfare Services, 1962. *Describes the history and expansion of volunteering in the United States, seeing the phenomenon as a "barometer of national vigor." Presents a brief classification of volunteers by the type of role they play.*

Cohen, Nathan E. "The Volunteer in Our Society." *Public Aid in Illinois* 31:8; May 1964. *General discussion of the voluntary roles of the citizen in American society.*

—————, editor. *The Citizen Volunteer: His Responsibility, Role and Opportunity in Modern Society.* New York: Harper and Bros., 1960. *Anthology drawing together material on specific programs and agencies, research data on volunteering from sociology and psychology, and philosophical/historical analyses of the role of voluntarism. Introduces the wide variety of approaches to the field of volunteering.*

Douglis, Marjorie. "The Worth of a Volunteer." *Women's Education* 6:8; March 1967. *Brief general discussion of the importance of volunteers to society.*

Glasser, Melvin A. *What Makes a Volunteer?* Public Affairs Pamphlet No. 224. New York: Public Affairs Committee, 1955. *Describes the fulfillment that volunteer service brings to the individual volunteer and the usefulness of his role to the agency he serves.*

Hassel, Leonard. "New Careers for Everyone." *Volunteer Administration* 1:18; Spring 1967. *Emphasizes the psychological wages the volunteer can earn. Urges a major new attempt to increase numbers and vary types of people who volunteer.*

Hubbell, Hulda. "What Educators Should Know About Volunteering." *Women's Education* 6:1, 7; March 1967. *Interprets the educational relevance of volunteer programs to professionals in the schools.*

Johns, Ray. *Confronting Organizational Change.* New York: Association Press, 1963. *Case-illustrated discussion of change in organizations in the field of social welfare. Discusses involvement and motivation of people for organizational goals.*

————. *Executive Responsibility: An Analysis of Executive Responsibility in the Work of Voluntary Community Social Welfare Organizations.* New York: Association Press, 1954. *Analyzes the roles and relationships of the agency executive. Discusses potential for integrating lay and professional experience in voluntary agency work.*

————, and DeMarche, David F. *Community Organization and Agency Responsibility.* New York: Association Press, 1951. *Examines the nature and function of communities and community organizations. Traces the history of community organizations and deals with subjects like interagency cooperation and the training of community organization workers.*

Johnson, Guion Griffis. "Exploring the Community's Volunteer Resources." *The Auxiliary Leader* 9:1-6; December 1968. *Brief survey of the importance of the volunteer role in American history and society. Some discussion of new sources of volunteer manpower that could be tapped by community agencies.*

————. *Volunteers in Community Service.* Prepared for North Carolina Council of Women's Organizations, Chapel Hill, North Carolina. Durham: Seeman Printery, 1967. *Based on extensive study of North Carolina volunteers and their supervisors. Comments on motivation, attitudes, experiences, and aspirations of volunteers and compares their attitudes on key questions about volunteer programs with those of supervisors of volunteers. Extensive bibliography.*

Knowles, Malcolm, editor. *Handbook of Adult Education in the United States.* Chicago: American Education Association of the United States of America, 1960. *Comprehensive anthology of* essays about the whole field of adult education. Includes several articles on the role of voluntary health and welfare organizations in adult education. Provides a context within which to view volunteer experiences as part of an educational process.

Lindeman, Eduard. *The Community: An Introduction to the Study of Community Leadership and Organization.* New York: Association Press, 1921. *Early discussion of community theory, with focus on citizen action and community agencies in their roles of meeting community needs.*

————. *The Meaning of Adult Education.* New York: New Republic, 1926. *Analyzes the needs of adults for individual self-expression and for collective social enterprise and focuses the role of adult education in these broad terms.*

————. *Social Discovery: An Approach to the Study of Functional Groups.* New York: Republic Publishing Co., 1925. *Discussion centers on methods of social research. Includes analysis of flexible techniques of research, such as group laboratories and use of participant observers. Particularly attends to redefinition of key terms in the group-leadership training field.*

Metcalfe, Henry C., and Urwick, L., editors. *Dynamic Administration: The Collected Papers of Mary Parker Follett.* New York: Harper and Bros., undated. *Published in the 1940's, this is an extensive collection of the papers of this social and organizational theorist and consultant, covering topics such as participation, leadership, authority, individualism, creative experience, and community process.*

Mills, Katherine A. "Volunteer Service Is Every Girl's Right." *Women's Education* 6:2; March 1967. *Explores the importance of service opportunities to the character growth of all girls.*

Naylor, Harriet H. *Volunteers Today: Finding, Training and Working with Them.* New York: Association Press, 1967. *General comprehensive summary of practical advice about the initiation and operation of volunteer programs. Analyzes societal trends and their implications for volunteering.*

Pereira, Joyce E. *A History of Volunteers in Social Welfare in the United States.* Unpublished master's thesis, Catholic University School of Social Work, 1947. *Divides the history of volunteers in social welfare work into periods and describes the characteristics of each era up through 1946.*

Rifield, Phyllis. "Volunteers Who Mean It: Today's Do-Gooders Have a Professional Commitment." *Mademoiselle* 64:118-19; December 1966. *Presents a model of volunteering for the new generation of young women. Describes the 1960's as the "Age of the Volunteer."*

Royal Bank of Canada Monthly Letter. "The Volunteer in Our Society." *Royal Bank of Canada Monthly Letter* 43:1-4; August 1962. *Affirmation of the values of volunteering both for the individual who offers his services and for the community that receives them.*

Schindler-Rainman, Eva. "The Era of the Volunteer Is Really Here." *MASV Journal* 1: 9-16; May 1970. (Michigan State University.) *Analyzes societal trends that are causing changes in the volunteer world and describes some of the new volunteer opportunities now available.*

Schindler-Rainman, Eva. "Are Volunteers Here To Stay?," *Mental Hygiene,* Vol. 55, No. 4, Oct. 1971 N.Y. *This paper reviews some trends and reasons why volunteers are indeed here to stay.*

Shriver, R. Sargent. "America's Amazing Volunteers." *Reader's Digest* 92:97-101; May 1968. *Provides enthusiasm and statistics about volunteers in various aspects of the War on Poverty program.*

Special Studies Project of the Rockefeller Brothers Fund. *The Power of the Democratic Idea.* Sixth Report. Garden City: Doubleday & Company, 1960. *Places the concept of volunteering and voluntary association in a broad theoretical framework and illuminates the role of voluntarism in a democratic society.*

Stenzel, Anne K., and Feeney, Helen M. *Volunteer Training and Development: A Manual for Community Groups.* New York: Seabury Press, 1968. *Comprehensive work covering most aspects of the theory and practice of running a good volunteer program. Special concentration on training and evaluation of volunteers. Takes a developmental approach to the role of the volunteer.*

Thursz, Daniel. "Some Views on Volunteers: Past Relic or Future Asset?" *Rehabilitation Record* 4; January-February 1963. (U.S. Department of Health, Education, and Welfare.) *Analyzes blocks that modern society places in the path of traditional volunteer roles and discusses the extent to which new forms have evolved or can evolve.*

Tocqueville, Alexis de. *Democracy in America.* New York: Vintage Books, 1955. 2 vols. *Classic analysis of American society in the nineteenth century. Points out the central role of voluntary activity and organization, both in the life of the individual citizen and in protecting the social fabric of democracy.*

Wilensky, Harold L., and Lebeaux, Charles N. *Industrial Society and Social Welfare.* Russell Sage Foundation. New York: Free Press, 1965. *Examines the social context of volunteering. Focuses on the evolution of welfare services in the United States and the role of the volunteer in welfare today.*

II. Program Settings

A. Education

Brenner, Marcella; Kear, Jeannette; and Wolfe, Bea. *Teacher Aides in Action in Elementary and Secondary Schools.* Follow-up of a project of the Model School Division of the Public Schools of the District of Columbia, conducted by the Washington School of Psychiatry. Washington, D.C.: Washington School of Psychiatry, 1969. *Examines attitudes of both aides and teachers and explores fully the operation and value of such a program.*

Gittelson, Natalie. "A Second Pair of Hands: School Volunteer Program." *New York Times Magazine,* March 19, 1967. p. 104 ff. *Analyzes the strengths and weaknesses of New York School Volunteer Program and in the process raises key issues about the role of white middle class volunteers in black and Spanish city ghettoes.*

Harre, David. "The Alley Library." *Top of the News* 24:208-11; January 1968. (Chicago: American Library Association.) *Describes the creation of a ghetto library to draw children who had had little positive relation with books or libraries before.*

Jamer, T. Margaret. *School Volunteers.* New York: Public Education Association, 1961. *Traces development of in-school volunteer program in the New York City school system that provided a model for what is now a national program. Describes procedures and includes job descriptions, sample forms, and research results.*

Janowitz, Gayle. *Helping Hands: Volunteer Work in Education.* Chicago: University of Chicago Press, 1965. *Provides an extensively detailed account of the operation of an after-school tutoring program and reflects on the role of such a program in the lives of ghetto children.*

Kohler, Mary. *Youth Tutoring Youth: It Worked.* New York: National Commission on Resources for Youth, 1968. *Describes experimental project in Newark and Philadelphia in which teens were paid to tutor children with learning difficulties.*

National School Volunteer Program. *Project Report.* New York: the Program, 1967. *Provides a history, description of operation, and evaluation of this expanding volunteer program. Covers the initial period from April 1964 to October 1967.*

Perkins, Bryce. *Getting Better Results from Substitutes, Teacher Aides and Volunteers.* Successful School Management Series. New Jersey: Prentice Hall, 1966. *Describes how volunteer programs in the schools may be initiated and managed. Gives examples of operating programs in a variety of local settings.*

Schindler-Rainman, Eva. "Toward Humane Management of School Volunteer Programs." *The Volunteer.* Columbus Public Schools, Vol. 1, No. 4, Spring 1975, Columbus Ohio, 1975. *This article gives ten characteristics of a humanely managed volunteer system.*

_____. "Trends, Societal Forces Affecting School Volunteers." *Newsletter. Spring 1975.* Los Angeles City Unified School District, Volunteer and Tutorial Program, Los Angeles, California. *Six major trends affecting volunteer programs are outlined and discussed.*

Tunick, Adele B. "New Opportunities—New Responsibilities." *1966 Annual Forum Proceedings.* New York: Association of Volunteer Bureaus of America, 1966. *Reports on a school volunteer program and the benefits derived from it by volunteers and students.*

B. Social Work

American Public Welfare Association. *Strengthening Public Welfare Services Through the Use of Volunteers.* Summary of material presented at an Institute sponsored by the Association. Chicago: the Association, 1960. *Reviews the whole context of public welfare work by agencies. Deals with such issues as the preparation of staff for acceptance of a volunteer program, the role of the board volunteer, types of services volunteers can render.*

Cain, Lillian Pike, and Epstein, Doris W. "The Utilization of Housewives as Volunteer Case Aides." *Social Casework* 48:282-

85; May 1967. *Describes program in Massachusetts in which untrained housewives were found to have considerable resources for successful work with the mentally ill.*

Chaskel, Ruth. *The Volunteer in Individualized Services.* New York: National Social Welfare Assembly, 1962. *Surveys the role volunteers play in the individual client services aspect of social work.*

Perlmutter, Felice, and Durham, Dorothy. "Using Teenagers To Supplement Casework Service." *Social Work* 10:41-46; April 1965. *Reviews a project in Champaign, Illinois, which uses teens in a therapeutic program. The project was especially designed to give support to teen workers and could involve all types of students, not just "high achievers."*

C. Welfare and Poverty

Family Service Association of America. *Use of Volunteers in Public Welfare.* New York: the Association, 1963. *Describes a series of pilot experimental projects in new or changed uses of volunteers by public welfare agencies. Reports on success and implications of the projects.*

Fenly, Robert F. "Volunteers in Social Welfare." *Social Work Yearbook 1957.* New York: National Association of Social Workers, 1957. pp. 592-98. *General survey and assessment of the role of volunteers in the field of social welfare work.*

Health and Welfare Council of the National Capital Area. *The Impact of a Developing Volunteer Program in a Public Welfare Institution for Dependent Children.* Washington, D.C.: the Council, August 1966. *Evaluates the effect of a volunteer program on a children's institution. Positive results have been achieved from a well-organized and diverse program.*

Nathan, Cynthia. "Why Does Public Welfare Need Volunteers?" *1968 Annual Forum Proceedings.* New York: Association of Volunteer Bureaus of America, 1968. pp. 36-41. *Presents the case for the role of the volunteer in governmental programs of social welfare.*

National Federation of Settlements and Neighborhood Centers. *100,000 Hours a Week: Volunteers in Service to Youth and*

Families. New York: the Federation, 1965. *Series of topics including description of tutoring programs and family service programs and discussion of the pros and cons of using indigenous volunteers in delinquency prevention programs.*

National Social Welfare Assembly. *The Volunteer's Contribution to the Solution of the Problem of Poverty.* New York: the Assembly, 1965. *Describes selected programs utilizing volunteers in fighting problems of poverty. Settings include VISTA, schools, social work, and psychiatry. Volunteers serve in paraprofessional capacities in several of the programs.*

Schindler-Rainman, Eva. "Connecting Low-Income People with Service Opportunities." *Creative Adaptation to Change.* Report of Seminar, Metropolitan Critical Areas Project. New York: Camp Fire Girls, 1965. pp. 87-93. *Describes specific examples of low-income people serving as volunteers in a variety of ways and settings.*

————. "A Dozen Musts in Working with the Disadvantaged." *Creative Adaptation to Change.* New York: Camp Fire Girls, 1965. pp. 95-96. *Suggests specific attitudes and techniques necessary for anyone working with deprived and disadvantaged people, with particular focus on involving volunteers.*

————. *Exploring Inner Space—What Are We Looking For and Why?* New York: National Social Welfare Assembly, 1964. *Outlines the first project in the United States in which a successful effort was made to recruit volunteers from poverty areas.*

————. "Leadership Training in Underdeveloped Neighborhoods." *Adult Leadership* 12:51-52; June 1963. (Chicago: Adult Education Association of the U.S.A.) *Describes sample leadership training activities that were tried in poverty areas, in an attempt to help local people become more active in their community.*

————. "Looking Backward, Looking Forward." *Innovation and Imagination for Youth.* New York: Camp Fire Girls, 1967. pp. 9-15. *Analyzes possibilities for expanded use of voluntary manpower. Focuses on extension of services of voluntary associations like the Camp Fire Girls to new people in new areas, especially poverty areas.*

————. "Recruiting and Training Indigenous Leaders in Low-Income Areas." *Creative Adaptation to Change.* New York: Camp Fire Girls, 1965. pp. 79-86. *Describes in detail recruitment and training techniques found successful in working with indigenous volunteer leaders in low-income areas in a number of cities throughout the United States.*

————. *A Unique New Venture.* Los Angeles: South Central Volunteer Bureau of Los Angeles, 1966. *Describes a volunteer-run Volunteer Bureau in inner-city Los Angeles which specializes in involvement and training of the indigenous poor in community and agency activity.*

————. *A Unique Venture Continued.* Los Angeles: South Central Volunteer Bureau of Los Angeles, 1967. *Further description of the inner-city Volunteer Bureau which works with volunteers and leaders in poverty areas. Lists what has been learned about the recruitment, training, and retention of indigenous volunteers.*

Schlosser, Don H. "Creative Use of Volunteers in Public Welfare." *1966 Annual Forum Proceedings.* New York: Association of Volunteer Bureaus of America, 1966. *Description of innovative ways in which volunteers can be and have been used in public welfare programs.*

U.S. Department of Health, Education, and Welfare, Project Head Start. *Volunteers in the Child Development Center Program.* Washington, D.C.: the Department, 1965. *Essentially a handbook on the use of volunteers in this particular aspect of the War on Poverty.*

U.S. Department of Health, Education, and Welfare, Welfare Administration, Bureau of Public Assistance. *Citizen Participation in Public Welfare Programs: Supplementary Services by Volunteers.* Washington, D.C.: Government Printing Office, 1956. *Provides guidelines for organizing volunteer programs in public welfare settings and presents the case for their use.*

D. Rehabilitation

Barker, G. H. *Volunteers in Corrections.* Portion of the report of the President's Commission on Law Enforcement and the Administration of Justice. Washington, D.C.: Government Printing Office, 1967. *Lengthy review of the role volunteers have played in publicly and privately sponsored correctional programs.*

Joint Commission on Correctional Manpower and Training. *Volunteers Look at Corrections.* Washington, D.C.: Government Printing Office, February 1969. *Report of a survey made by Louis*

Harris and Associates of volunteers in the corrections field. Covers what work they do, who they are, why they volunteer, and their attitudes toward their volunteer roles and organizations. Explores the ramifications of these findings for the corrections field.

Levin, Stanley. *Volunteers in Rehabilitation.* Goodwill Industries, Washington, D.C., 1973. *An outstanding series covering volunteers in rehabilitation facilities serving handicapped and disadvantaged persons.*

Royal Oak (Michigan) Municipal Court Probation Department. *Concerned Citizens and a City Criminal Court.* Royal Oak: the Department, undated. *Presents a history of the origin, financing, and operation of an unusual volunteer program in this Michigan court system.*

Scheier, Ivan H. *Using Volunteers in Court Settings: A Manual for Volunteer Probation Programs.* U.S. Department of Health, Education, and Welfare, Social and Rehabilitation Service, Office of Juvenile Delinquency and Youth Development. Washington, D.C.: the Department, 1969. *Provides guidance in the initiation and operation of a volunteer program in the court system. Includes suggestions for evaluation of programs, their financing, and public relations, as well as sections on recruitment, training, and placement.*

————. *Volunteer Programs in Courts: Collected Papers on Productive Programs.* U.S. Department of Health, Education, and Welfare, Social and Rehabilitation Service, Office of Juvenile Delinquency and Youth Development. Washington, D.C.: the Department, 1969. *Discusses various roles volunteers can play within the court structure: probation officers, tutors, discussion group leaders, hosts of homes away from home. Includes documented accounts of actual programs.*

Volunteers! And the Rehabilitation of Criminal Offenders. Volunteers in Probation. Royal Oak, Michigan, 1970. *A report of a conference that analyzed the utilization of volunteers working with offenders.*

E. Mental Health

American Psychiatric Association. *The Volunteer and the Psychiatric Patient.* Report of the Conference on Volunteer Services to Psychiatric Patients. Washington, D.C.: the Association, 1959. *A developmental approach emphasizing real involvement of and appreciation for volunteers in psychiatric settings. Includes data on uses of volunteers throughout the country and an extensive annotated bibliography covering the entire field of mental health volunteers.*

Cummins, Sister Mary Josephine. *College Student Volunteers in State Mental Hospitals.* National Institute of Mental Health, Citizen Participation Branch, Public Health Service Publication No. 1752. Washington, D.C.: Public Health Service, 1967. *Brief report of results of a survey of mental hospitals for data regarding their use of volunteers. Gives numerical data on hospitals having programs and on types of uses of volunteers. Lists names of hospitals having volunteer programs.*

Eliasoph, Eugene. "The Use of Volunteers As Case Aides in a Treatment Setting." *Social Casework* 40:141-44; March 1959. *Describes possibilities for using volunteers in therapeutic setting and cites case examples of successful experiences.*

Frank, Marjorie H. *Volunteer Participation in Psychiatric Hospital Services.* New York: National Committee for Mental Hygiene, 1950. *Overview of how to run a volunteer program in a psychiatric hospital. Includes resource materials and outlines for training and programing.*

————, and Kilpatrick, O. Arnold, editors. *Volunteers in Mental Hospitals.* New York: National Association for Mental Health, 1960. *Reviews nature of volunteer work in mental institutions throughout the country.*

Milne, James. "Voluntary Service and the Mental Hospital," *World Mental Health* 8:64-70; 1956. *Describes the effects of volunteers on patients in mental hospitals. The effects are seen to be positive: volunteers help patients achieve greater personal integration and prevent desocialization.*

National Association for Mental Health. *Volunteer Services in Mental Hospitals.* Report of the Institute for Directors of Volunteer Services in Mental Hospitals. New York: the Association, 1960. *Designed to assist directors of volunteers in mental hospitals in the philosophy, interpretation, and operation of their program.*

————. *Youth Volunteers in Mental Hospitals.* New York: the Association, 1962. *Seeks to guide NAMH chapters in providing liaison between hospitals and groups of youth volunteers. Brief description of two types of programs.*

National Institute of Mental Health, Citizen Participation Branch. *College Student Volunteer in State Mental Hospitals.* Public Health Service Publication No. 1752. Washington, D.C.: Public Health Service, 1967. *Briefly reports results of a survey of mental hospitals for data regarding their use of volunteers. Lists hospitals having volunteer programs.*

Sharp, Agnes Arminda. *Why Volunteers?* Springfield, Illinois: State Department of Mental Health, 1964. *Promotional piece advocating use of volunteers in mental health centers.*

F. Hospitals

American Hospital Association. *Hospital Auxiliaries and Volunteers.* Report Series No. 3. Chicago: the Association, 1963. *Report of a survey conducted by AHA in 1962 on volunteer and auxiliary programs. Organized by geography, size of hospital, type of volunteer service, etc.*

————. *The Teen-Age Volunteer in the Hospital and Other Health Care Facilities.* Chicago: the Association, 1959, 1964. *Describes standards for service by teen-agers in hospitals and emphasizes the importance of using the service as an opportunity for career tryout with the hope of recruiting more professional and service personnel to careers in the hospital field.*

————. *The Volunteer in the Hospital.* Revised edition. Chicago: the Association, 1963. *Describes approved procedures for developing a volunteer program in a hospital. Includes brief unannotated bibliography of volunteering in hospital settings.*

————. *The Volunteer in Long-Term Care.* Chicago: the Association, 1968. *Practical guide for volunteer programs in hospital settings. Includes extensive annotated bibliography on use of volunteers in various medical settings.*

Binkley, Lois; Podolinsky, Agnes; and von Richter, Frank. "Fewer Auxiliaries and Volunteers Are Providing More—and More Kinds—of Services." *Hospitals* 42:60-64; March 16, 1968. *Reports results of 1965 survey similar to one conducted in 1962 by the American Hospital Association. Highlights the importance of volunteers in bridging the gap between supply and demand in professional services in hospitals. Provides descriptive data on volunteers and volunteer programs.*

Hartog, Jan de. *The Hospital.* New York: Atheneum Press, 1964. *Personal narration of experiences of this novelist as one of a small group of volunteer orderlies in a hospital in Texas.*

White, Ferris, Jr. "Strengths and Weaknesses of Volunteers and Volunteer Systems." *Modern Hospital* 80:98-102; 1953. *Analysis by a Chicago management consultant of the permeating and consistent patterns and processes of most volunteer programs, including hospitals.*

G. International

Biddle, William W. and Loureide J. *Encouraging Community Development: A Training Guide for Local Workers.* New York: Holt, Rinehart & Winston, 1968. *Focuses on the role of the partially paid volunteer in government programs like VISTA and the Peace Corps. The book is based in the community development field and views the compensated volunteer as the opening manifestation of a new profession.*

Delano, William A. "Volunteers and Development." *International Development Review* 8:2-7; September 1966. *Lauds the important role of volunteers in development work throughout the world, particularly in meeting the need for mid-level management. Focuses on volunteer programs of the International Secretariat for Volunteer Service (ISVS).*

Fuchs, Lawrence A. *The Volunteer Aspect of Being a Peace Corps Volunteer.* Harriet Lowenstein Goldstein Series, The Volunteer in America. No. 12, Papers in Social Welfare, Issue No. 2. Waltham, Mass.: Brandeis University, undated. *Examines the voluntary component of the Peace Corps volunteer's motivation and role.*

Stein, Morris I. *Volunteers for Peace: The First Group of Peace Corps Volunteers in a Rural Community Development Program in Colombia, South America.* New York: John Wiley & Sons, 1966. *Chronicles the history of the first group of Peace Corps volunteers. Includes extensive statistical data on their training, selection, motivation, and effectiveness.*

H. Citizen Participation Models of Community Development

Johnson, Guion Griffis. *Volunteers in Community Service.* North Carolina Council of Womens Organizations, Inc., Chapel Hill, N.C., 1967.

National Assembly for Social Policy and Development. *New Trends in Citizen Involvement and Participation.* New York: the Assembly, 1956. *Series of papers concerning new citizen participation models for social change. Includes case histories of projects. Proposes that as serious and expert an approach be made to the role of citizen as is now made to the career role.*

National Federation of Settlements and Neighborhood Centers. *Dynamics of Citizen Participation.* New York: the Federation, undated. *Published in the late 1950's, this is a community theory approach to finding leaders and operating programs of broad-scale involvement in inner city settings. Some discussion of interagency participation, its goals and values.*

————. *Organizing Neighbors To Act on Their Own.* New York: the Federation, 1957. *Summary of conference on the improvement of citizen participation, sponsored by the Federation. Provides guidelines for improving citizen participation in urban areas.*

Schindler-Rainman, Eva. "The Potentials of Volunteers in Urban Planning." *Next Steps in Strengthening Social Components of Urban Planning.* (Edited by L. K. Northwood.) New York: Wiley Press, 1970. *Suggests a variety of ways to utilize volunteers in urban planning in order to provide broader citizen participation.*

Schindler-Rainman, Eva. "Community Development Through Laboratory Education." *The Laboratory Method of Learning and Changing: Theory and Application.* Ed. Bradford L., Benne K., Gibb J., Lippitt, R. Science and Behavior Books, Palo Alto, Calif., 1975.

Spiegel, Hans B. C., Editor. "Decentralization." *Citizen Participation in Urban Development,* Volume III. NTL Learning Resources Corporation, Fairfax, Va., 1974.

Spiegel, Hans B. C., editor. *Concepts and Issues.* (Vol. 1 of *Citizen Participation in Urban Development.*) Washington, D.C.: NTL Institute for Applied Behavioral Science, Center for Community Affairs, 1968. *Collection of readings focused on citizen participation, especially the participation of the poor in governmental programs of urban renewal, war on poverty, etc. Includes bibliography on the literature of the field.*

I. Miscellaneous

Committee of Correspondence. *Volunteers Can Make the Difference.* New York: the Committee, 1964. *Collection of essays de-*

scribing the impact of volunteers on a variety of community service programs.

DeGrazie, Alfred, editor. *Grass Roots Private Welfare.* New York: New York University Press, 1957. *Presents winning essays from a competition sponsored by the Foundation for Voluntary Welfare. Essays describe various private community volunteer programs organized to combat community problems. Several discuss the role of voluntarism in general.*

Levin, Stanley; Parisien, Noel; and Thursz, Daniel. *A Handbook on Volunteers in Army Community Services.* Prepared at the University of Maryland Center for the Study of Voluntarism. Washington, D.C.: Department of the Army, Human Resources Research Office, 1969. *Detailed outline of how to institute and maintain an effective volunteer program. Includes material on training, selection, placement, evaluation, recognition, etc., specially designed for the Army setting.*

Levine, Margaret. "Volunteers Serve New York State." *Facts for Filing.* Albany: Women's Unit, Executive Chamber, 1968. *Review of what volunteers are doing throughout New York State in mental hygiene, social services, senior citizens programs, and the development of equal opportunity.*

Michigan Department of Social Services, Volunteer Services Project. *Volunteer Services Pilot Project.* Lansing: the Department, 1967. *Thorough discussion of inception and operation of an unusual family-to-family volunteer program in which whole family units offer to serve as helpers/sponsors to other family units in struggles with jobs, welfare programs, social life, etc.*

National Commission on Resources for Youth. *Selected Youth Participation Projects.* Prepared for the Joint Commission on the Mental Health of Children. New York: National Commission on Resources for Youth, 1968. *Documents the great variety and effectiveness of programs to involve young volunteers. Includes several case studies in depth, surveys numerous projects briefly. Tells whom to contact for further information about each project.*

Schindler-Rainman, Eva, and Lippitt, Ronald. "Hopes and Prospects in Adult Education: Working With People Whom We Forgot." *Interpersonal Development.* S. Karger, Basel, Switzerland. 4:107-119 (1973-74). *This article deals with adults who have been overlooked as clients of adult education activities. It gives ideas of how to include these persons.*

Schumacher, Marjorie. *Extending Services Through the Use of Volunteers.* New York: Planned Parenthood, World Population, 1968. *Reviews the experience of this organization in granting increasing responsibility to volunteers over the years. Concludes that despite problems the effort to train volunteers to cope with ever higher levels of responsibility is well worthwhile.*

Telephone Pioneers of America. *Pioneer Progress, 1967-1968.* Annual Report. New York: the Pioneers, 1968. *Reviews what has been done by the service organization of a particular industry through voluntary social welfare programs.*

III. Functional Aspects of Volunteer Programs

A. Motivation, Recruitment, Placement, and Recognition

Adult Education Association. *Working with Volunteers.* Leadership Pamphlet No. 10. Washington, D.C.: the Association, 1956. *Overview of all aspects of a program for volunteers, from recruitment and motivation to placement and supervision.*

American Red Cross. *Placing Volunteers.* Washington, D.C.: the Red Cross, 1965. *One of a series of pamphlets dealing with the practical aspects of operating a volunteer program. Others include topics such as personnel practices, interviewing, basic training, and principles of volunteer service.*

Auerbach, Arnold J. "Aspirations of Power People and Agency Goals." *Social Work* 6:66-73; January 1961. *Examines the motives that lead people to seek significant roles in voluntary community service and attempts to draw implications for the improved operation of agency boards.*

Barclay, D. "Filling the Need To Feel Needed." *New York Times Magazine,* March 29, 1959. p. 42. *Discusses the psychological and social needs that motivate people to do volunteer work.*

Coleman, Jules. "Motivations of the Volunteer in the Health and Welfare Fields." *Mental Hygiene* 41:218; April 1957. *Reports on the crucial factors involved in the motivation of volunteers in these major voluntary action fields.*

Colmen, Joseph G. "Volunteerism: A Constructive Outlet for Youthful Energy." *Journal of Marriage and the Family* 27:171-75; May 1965. *Advocates expansion of a model of volunteerism that, like the Peace Corps, appeals to such developmental goals as testing of self, exploration of values and structures of society, and fulfillment of independence.*

Girl Scouts of the United States of America. *Recruiting, Selecting and Placing Volunteers.* New York: the Girl Scouts, 1960. *A practical guide for recruiters of volunteers.*

Schindler-Rainman, Eva. "Why Do People Volunteer?" *Community Organization Papers.* National Conference on Social Welfare. New York: Columbia University Press, 1959. pp. 127-33. *Describes some of the motivations of people to volunteer, and some of the reasons why they do.*

Volunteer Recognition. Publication of the National Center for Voluntary Action, Washington, D.C., 1973. *In this booklet seven leaders in the volunteer field write about ways to recognize volunteers. Also included are both formal and informal approaches to recognition.*

B. Training, Supervision, and Administration

Abrams, Percy. "Education of the Volunteer." *Youth Leader's Digest* 26:273-78; June-September 1964. *Describes the variety of training techniques available and emphasizes the need for continuing training and supervision of volunteers.*

Christ, Jacob. "Volunteer Training as an Education." *Mental Hygiene* 51:433-39; July 1967. *Advocates a broad and continuing program of training for volunteers, including a well-rounded set of emotional and intellectual learning experiences.*

Health and Welfare Council of the National Capital Area, Volunteer Services Branch. *How To Work with Volunteers.* Demonstration training course for staff. Washington, D.C.: the Council, 1962. *Transcribed summaries of a course prepared through the pooled resources of many agencies and educational institutions for the training of personnel who work with volunteers.*

Larkin, Kathleen Ormsby. *For Volunteers Who Interview.* Chicago: Volunteer Bureau, Welfare Council of Metropolitan Chicago, 1968. *A guide for volunteers whose job is to interview prospective volunteers.*

Lippitt, Ronald and Schindler-Rainman, Eva. "Designing for Participative Learning and Changing." *The Laboratory Method of Learning and Changing: Theory and Application,* edited by Bradford, L., Benne K., Gibb J., and Lippitt R. Science and Behavior Books, Palo Alto, Calif., 1975.

————. "Designing Learning Experiences Planning Charts." Organizational Renewal, Inc., Washington, D.C., 1973. *Here are two useful frameworks for persons planning training. It gives a way to organize your planning.*

Naylor, Harriet H. *Volunteers Today: Finding, Training and Working with Them.* New York: Association Press, 1967. *Comprehensive general summary of practical advice about the initiation and operation of volunteer programs. Analyzes societal trends and their implications for volunteering.*

Schindler-Rainman, Eva and Lippitt, Ronald. *Developing Your Volunteer Community.* A Multi-Media Package developed with XICOM, Inc., New York. Available through NTL Learning Resources Corp., Fairfax, Va., 1975.

_____. *Team Training for Community Change: Concepts, Goals, Strategies and Skills.* University Extension, University of California, Riverside, 1972. NTL-Learning Resources Corp., Fairfax, Va., 1972. *This publication focuses on the art and skills of training teams to function in the community. Many specific training techniques are described in detail.*

Research and Development, National Council of YMCAs. *Training Volunteer Leaders.* A Handbook to Train Volunteers and Other Leaders of Program Groups. YMCA, New York, N.Y., 1974. *A loose leaf handbook of excellent items covering: training the trainer, establishing a climate for learning and training methods to help leaders organize groups and establish good communication.*

Scheier, Ivan. *Frontier 13: People Approach Systems of Volunteer Involvement: Noah and Minimax,* National Information Center on Volunteerism, Boulder, Colorado, 1974. *An exciting new development from the Center giving broader directions to volunteer job definition processes and involvement of wider ranges of people, suitable to all areas of volunteer service, and applicable to program planning as well as recruiting.*

_____. *Frontier 11: Orienting Staff to Volunteers,* National Information Center on Volunteerism, Boulder, Colorado, 1972. *This publication provides background, insights, and practical strategies for dealing with staff resistance to volunteers.*

Schindler-Rainman, Eva. *Trainers in Action.* New York: Camp Fire Girls, 1969. *Designed to guide trainers of adult leaders of Camp Fire Girl groups.*

Spergel, Irving. "Role Behavior and Supervision of the Untrained Group Worker." *Social Work* 7:69-76; July 1962. *Stresses that organizations must take account of prior attitudes that influence untrained workers in their group programs. Careful orientation is needed to achieve successful meshing of individual worker with the needs of the agency and the group.*

Stenzel, Anne K., and Feeney, Helen M. *Volunteer Training and Development: A Manual for Community Groups.* New York: Seabury Press, 1968. *Comprehensive work covering aspects of the theory and practice of running a good volunteer program. Special concentration on training and evaluation of volunteers. Takes a developmental approach to the role of the volunteer.*

United Community Services Volunteer Bureau of Omaha. *Creative Supervision of Volunteers: A Conference for Career Supervisors, Volunteer Supervisors, Lay Workers.* Omaha, Nebraska: the Bureau, 1964. *Proceedings of the conference shed light on the general principles of supervision, with particular reference to the motivation, retention, and growth of volunteer workers.*

C. Volunteer–Staff Relations

Brown, W. L. "Unearthing an Organization's Hidden Perceptions: Relationships Between Volunteers and Staff." *Adult Leadership* 12:239; February 1964. *Describes the importance of discovering and sharing basic attitudes of volunteers and staff toward each other and their organization as a basis for improved teamwork.*

Council of National Organizations for Adult Education. *Probing Volunteer-Staff Relations.* New York: Association Press, 1963. *Provides a kit of instruments for organizational self-analysis of relations between staff and volunteers. Concentrates on comparative perceptions of the two groups about their organization as a way of increasing communication between the groups.*

Monroe, Donald and Keith. *How To Succeed in Community Service.* Philadelphia: J. B. Lippincott Co., 1962. *How-to manual, unusual in that it is aimed at the volunteer. Offers advice and guidance on how to relate to professional staff and how to make oneself useful and effective as a volunteer.*

National Conference on Social Welfare. *Volunteer and Professional Staff: 1962 Models.* Summary of 1962 Conference held at Columbus, Ohio. New York: the Conference, 1962. *Transcriptions of papers read and discussions held on the issues surrounding relationships of volunteers and professional staff.*

National Social Welfare Assembly. *The Significance of the Volunteer on the American Scene.* New York: the Assembly, 1963. *Dis-*

cussion of relationships and differences between volunteers and professionals, the role of volunteers in several fields of social work, and the needs for recruitment and retention of volunteers.

Naylor, Harriet H. "Varying Perceptions: Good Working Relationships Between Staff and Volunteers." *Adult Education* 14:137-41; Spring 1964. *Discusses the importance of sharing viewpoints between staff and volunteers in facilitating an effective relationship. Offers pointers about ways to improve the teamwork of the two groups.*

Pernell, Ruby B. "Professional and Volunteer Workers in Traditional Youth-Serving Agencies." *Social Work* 2:63-67; January 1957. *Discusses the problems and possibilities inherent in personnel distribution and assignment, particularly in terms of differences between volunteers and staff.*

Royfe, Ephraim H. "The Role of a Social Worker in a Big Brother Agency." *Social Casework* 41:139-44; March 1960. Case study *of an organization that has had to deal with acceptance by volunteers of the addition of social workers to the organization staff. This pattern, which was common to many organizations at an earlier period of history, has been examined in reverse for many organizations in the contemporary era.*

D. Decision Makers

Houle, Cyril D. *The Effective Board.* New York: Association Press, 1960. *Based on a training program for members of a city-wide board, this book seeks to set forth key principles for effective work by the volunteer board of an agency.*

National Information Bureau. *The Volunteer Board Member in Philanthropy.* New York: the Bureau, 1968. *Attempts to orient the board member to his role, both its opportunities and its dangers. Includes bibliography.*

Schmidt, William L. *The Executive and the Board in Social Welfare.* Cleveland: Howard Allen, 1959. *Outlines a possible form of organization that could contribute to effective working relations between board and executive. Gives practical guidance on how the board-executive relationship may be made fruitful and effective.*

Sorenson, Roy. *The Art of Board Membership.* New York: Association Press, 1950. *Extensive analysis of the board member's role and function from both the management and social work frames of reference. Provides guidance for the new and old board member alike.*

―――. *How To Be a Board or Committee Member.* New York: Association Press, 1953. *Brief popular version of the above work.*

Trecker, Harleigh B. *Building the Board.* New York: Natonal Public Relations Council of Health and Welfare Services, 1954. *Thorough presentation of the recruitment, training, and utilization of creative board members by voluntary organizations.*

E. The Future

Cleveland, Harlan. "The Decision Makers." *The Center Magazine,* Vol. VI, No. 5, Sept./Oct. 1973. Center for the Study of Democratic Institution, Santa Barbara, Calif., 1973. *This article clarifies alternative organizational models where decision making and communication become more horizontal, open and decentralized. There are many implications for organizations utilizing volunteers.*

Fox, Robert, Lippitt, Ronald, Schindler-Rainman, Eva. *Towards A Humane Society: Images of Potentiality,* NTL Learning Resources Corp., Fairfax, Va., 1973. *Realism in future and goal planning is the essence of this book. Three cases, The Humanizing School, The Socializing Community, The Volunteer Community, focus on the images of how these systems can be humanized. Two chapters of examples and specific descriptions useful in designing individual, group and organizational training activities on goal setting and future planning are included.*

Gappert, Gary. "Post Affluence: The Turbulent Transition to a Post-Industrial Society." *The Futurist.* Vol. VIII, No. 5, Oct., 1974, Washington, D.C. *This article deals with changes in Society that will occur, including the post industrial worker, the changing family, redistribution of income, population mobility and the growth of the leisure ethic.*

Little, Dennis reviews "Post Industrial Society and What It May Mean" by Daniel Bell. *The Futurist,* Vol. II, No. 6, Dec. 1973. Washington, D.C. *The review of Mr. Bell's book focuses on the shift from an agricultural and manufacturing society to one of human services. The implications of the changes inherent in this shift are carefully analyzed and discussed.*

Research and Development Division, National Council of YMCAs. *VOLUNTARISM: Confrontation and Opportunity,* YMCA, New

York, 1975. *Drs. C. Carey, J. Hardy, R. Lippitt, E. Schindler-Rainman analyze and describe the history of volunteerism in the YMCA, and suggests emerging challenges and selected images for future action.*

Schindler-Rainman, Eva and Lippitt, Ronald. "The Shape of the Future is Already Here." *The Girl Scout Leader Magazine.* Jan.-Feb. 1974, New York. *An article discussing future trends with specific implications and strategy action examples for adult volunteers and youth members.*

IV. Human Resources Available for Volunteer Work

A. Youth

Eberly, Donald J. "Service Experience and Educational Growth." *Educational Record* 49:197-205; Spring 1968. *Pleads the case for the recognition by institutions of higher education of the importance and value of service experiences for college students.*

————, editor. *National Service: A Report of a Conference.* New York: Russell Sage Foundation, 1968. *Examination of the concept of national service for all young people. Analyzes such topics as manpower needs to meet social objectives, and social problems where service is needed. Proposes national service as a design for solving social problems, as an alternative or complement to volunteering.*

National Social Welfare Assembly. *Youth in Community Affairs.* New York: the Assembly, 1958. *Summary of a consultation of youth leaders which attempted to gain insight into key factors motivating youth to participate in service roles.*

————. *Youth Takes the Field.* New York: the Assembly, 1962. *Aimed at teen-agers, this pamphlet describes areas where they may seek involvement in social service and provides practical guidelines for self-assessment regarding such involvement.*

B. Elderly

Johnson, Keith. "Foster Grandparents for Emotionally Disturbed Children." *Children* 14:46-52; March-April 1967. *Reviews the OEO program in which poverty-level elderly volunteers are paid minimum compensation to work with children. Relevant both to indigenous volunteer programs and to the newer concepts of the partially compensated volunteer.*

Rosenblatt, Aaron. "Interest of Older Persons in Volunteer Activities." *Social Work* 11:87-94; July 1966. *Reports a survey of 250 elderly persons regarding their interest in and skills for volunteer work. General conclusion: although most were interested, few had extensive skills. Therefore, special training and attention were prerequisite to real use of this particular group.*

Worthington, Gladys. "Older Persons as Community Service Volunteers." *Social Work* 8:71-75; October 1963. *Analyzes the problems and possibilities of using elderly persons as a new volunteer pool.*

C. Men

Danielson, John M. "Men in a Women's World." *Auxiliary Leader* 3:9-11; August 1962. *Describes the role of male volunteers in the traditionally feminine hospital volunteer setting.*

Fenn, Dan H., Jr. "Executives as Community Volunteers," Harvard Business Review, March/April 1971 pp. 4-16, 156-159.

French, Lynn. "New Fields for Men Volunteers." *Hospitals* 36: 49-51; October 1962. (American Hospital Association.) *Emphasizes the widening possibilities for use of male volunteers in the health care setting.*

Montmorency, Arthur F. "There's a Man in the House and a Woman Out of the Home." *Proceedings of 1964 Annual Workshop.* New York: Association of Volunteer Bureaus of America, 1964. *Discusses the roles of men and women both in the home and in community service, with special emphasis on the new roles of male volunteers.*

Rezak, Nicholas. "Trends in the Participation of Businessmen in Local Voluntary Affairs." *Sociology and Social Research* 48:289-300; April 1964. *Deals with the participation patterns of businessmen in the voluntary agencies and associations which handle so many social and welfare problems in the community.*

United Community Funds and Councils of America. *The Businessman in Community Planning.* New York: the United Community Funds and Councils, 1959. *Reports the results of a study of what businessmen respond to, like, and require in their participation in community service. Provides guidelines for recruiting and maintaining this manpower group in volunteer and board roles.*

D. Women

Bolger, Eugenie, "Take it Out of My Salary: Volunteers on the Prestige Circuit," *Ms. Magazine*, New York, Feb. 1975. *An article critical of women doing volunteer work and some of the problems they run into including resistant staff, needs for status, menial jobs, and sexism.*

Gold, Doris B. "Women and Voluntarism." *Woman in Sexist Society.* Editors Vivian Gornick and Barbara K. Moran, Basic Books, Inc. New York, 1971, pp. 384-400.

Horner, Matina. "Femininity and Successful Achievement: A Basic Inconsistency in Feminine Personality and Conflict." Ed. Judith M. Bardwick, Elizabeth Dowan, Matina Horner and David Gutman. Brook/Cole Publishing Co., Belmont, Calif., 1970.

Loeser, Herta. *Women, Work and Volunteering.* Beacon Press, Boston, 1974. *This is an up to date book that makes a case for volunteering but sets this case in the present time and takes into account opposition to voluntarism as well as woman's changing roles.*

New York Times. "Wanted: Educated Women To Start or Return to Work in Community Service." *New York Times,* October 1, 1966. p. 20. *Outlines the need and opportunity for women in volunteer service roles and makes a particular appeal to the educated woman who may also be attracted to a work career.*

NOW—Resolution on Voluntarism, presented at the 5th National Conference, Los Angeles, Calif., September 1971, NOW (National Organization for Women), Chicago, Ill.

_____. "Volunteer—Why Not? Analysis and Answers," Chicago Task Force for Women and Volunteerism, 1973, NOW, Chicago, Ill.

Rothe, MaryLou, and Newark, Christine. "Homemakers in Voluntary Community Activities." *Marriage and Family Living* 20: 175-78; May 1958. *Traces the trends in married women's participation in the labor and volunteer labor forces of the American economy since 1890. Observes that women still see volunteering as part of this role, even with their increased participation in the paid labor force, but that their motivation now is more recreation- and self-improvement—oriented, and less service-oriented.*

Sanborn, Margaret A. and Bird, Caroline. "The Big Giveaway, What Volunteer Work is Worth." *Ms. Magazine,* New York, Feb. 1975. *The authors are critical of volunteers performing jobs that paid workers should do, that there are few income tax deductions for volunteers, and that often insurance for volunteers while volunteering is inadequate or lacking.*

Schindler-Rainman, Eva. "Opportunity — An Answer to NOW," *Voluntary Action News,* National Center for Voluntary Action, Washington, D.C., December 1971.

Schindler-Rainman, Eva. "Surfacing—An Overlooked Minority?" *Adult Leadership* 18: 305-306, 324-25; April 1970. *Describes the emerging creative role of women in both the workaday and the volunteer worlds.*

Strauss, Ellen Sulzberger. "In Defense of Unpaid Labor." *Ms. Magazine,* New York, February 1975. *The writer points out the benefits to persons from volunteering, the changes that are taking place in the volunteer world, and the need for volunteers as participants in a democratic society.*

Women's Yellow Pages. Ed. Carol Freedman Edry, Ginnie Goulet. Women's Collective, Cambridge, Boston, 1974.

E. The Poor

Camp Fire Girls, Inc. *Innovation and Imagination for Youth.* Report of Seminar IV, Metropolitan Critical Areas Project. New York: Camp Fire Girls, 1967. *Documents in a workshop type of report the efforts of this organization to apply its traditional program of volunteer leadership to the new challenges of an urban environment. Includes discussion of use of indigenous volunteers.*

Coggs, Pauline R., and Robinson, Vivian R. "Training Indigenous Community Leaders for Employment in Social Work." *Social Casework* 48: 278-81; May 1967. *Sample of numerous articles on training indigenous personnel for paraprofessional jobs in social work. Not directly volunteer work, these jobs represent a gray area between new partially compensated volunteer roles and paid paraprofessional roles in poverty areas.*

Freeman, Lucy. "Biennial Conference Roundup Report: Citizen Participation." *Public Welfare* 14: 28-29; January 1956. *A brief look at the use of clients as volunteers in public welfare programs. Advice on how to make it work.*

Jackson, Nelson C. "The Use of Indigenous Volunteers from Minority and Culturally Deprived Groups." *Social Work Practices— 1964.* New York: National Conference on Social Welfare, 1964. *Examines the pros and cons of the use of minority and "culturally deprived" groups in volunteer roles in which they have not traditionally been involved.*

National Social Welfare Assembly. *Employing Staff from the Client Group: New Developments.* Presented at the annual forum of the National Conference on Social Welfare, 1966. New York: the Assembly, 1966. *Describes involvement of indigenous personnel in paraprofessional roles in social casework. Holds relevance for issues regarding paid volunteers, particularly indigenous poor.*

Pearl, Arthur, and Riessman, Frank. *New Careers for the Poor: The Non-Professional in Human Services.* New York: Free Press, Macmillan Co., 1965. *Analyzes the possibilities for use of the poor in paraprofessional roles in community service. Indirectly bears on the increased use of indigenous volunteers who are partially compensated.*

Piven, Frances. "Participation of Residents in Neighborhood Community Action Programs." *Social Work* 11: 73-80; January 1966. *Highlights the need for careful planning to overcome obstacles to community participation on the part of lower-income residents. Emphasizes that needs and skills of this group are different from those of traditional middle-income volunteers.*

Richards, Catherine V., and Polansky, Norman A. "Reaching Working Class Youth Leaders." *Social Work* 4:31-39; October 1959. *Report of a study commissioned by the Girl Scouts because of their need to improve recruitment of indigenous leadership in poverty and working class areas. Suggests approaches that may be effective.*

Robinson, James. "Summary and Recommendations from the Consultation on Minority Participation in Voluntary Service Programs." *Volunteer Digest* 5:1-4; November 1968. *These are the results of a conference convened by the Commission on Youth Service Projects. Forces favoring and inhibiting minority groups' participation in volunteer service are discussed.*

Schindler-Rainman, Eva. "The Poor and the PTA." *PTA Magazine* 61:4-7; April 1967. *Surveys the obstacles to involvement of the poor in typical PTA programs and suggests possible ways to increase their participation through changes in the organization.*

————, and Lippitt, Ronald. "What We Have Learned from Working with the Poor." *Human Relations Training News* 13:1-3; 1969. *Analyzes lessons the poor have taught to middle class groups working with them. Highlights creative differences in family relationships, use of time, expressiveness, etc.*

V. Voluntary Associations

American Medical Association. *Directory of National Voluntary Health Organizations.* Chicago: the Association, published annually. *Handbook for physicians and medical agencies, listing voluntary health organizations in the United States.*

Babchuk, Nicholas, and Edwards, John N. "Voluntary Association and the Integration Hypothesis." *Sociological Inquiry* 35:149-62; April 1965. *Reviews substance of the traditional theory that voluntary associations play an integrative function in complex societies. Reviews the literature on the subject and attempts to highlight factors not generally discussed therein.*

————, and Gordon, C. Wayne. *The Voluntary Association in the Slum.* Nebraska University Studies, N.S. No. 27. Lincoln, Nebraska: University of Nebraska Press, 1962. *Examination of the voluntary association in a slum setting. Traces the role of such organizations, usually associated with middle class life, in the lives of minorities and the poor.*

Barber, Bernard. "Participation and Mass Apathy in Associations." *Studies in Leadership.* (Edited by Alvin W. Gouldner.) New York: Harper Brothers, 1950. pp. 477-504. *Classic study analyzes the conflicts between the democratic value of citizen participation in voluntary associations and the apathy-producing realities of formal bureaucratic organizations. Documents the central facts that most citizens hold no memberships in voluntary organizations and that most organizations are run by oligarchies.*

Birnbaum, Max. "Adult Education in General Voluntary Organizations." *Handbook of Adult Education in the United States.* (Edited by Malcolm Knowles.) Chicago: Adult Education Association, 1960. pp. 378-92. *Deals with the role of voluntary organizations in informal adult education.*

Carter, Richard. *The Gentle Legions.* Garden City: Doubleday and Co., 1961. *Discusses the history and development of the various major voluntary health organizations, stressing their unique and important role in American public health.*

Freeman, Howard E.; Novak, Edwin; and Reeder, Leo G. "Correlates of Membership in Voluntary Associations." *American Soci-*

ological Review 22:528-33; October 1957. *Attempts to find predictive variables, other than socioeconomic status, for voluntary association membership.*

Glaser, William A., and Sills, Donald L. *The Government of Associations: Selections from the Behavioral Sciences.* New York: Bedminster Press, 1966. *Comprehensive analysis of voluntary associations in their various functional, historical, and organizational aspects. Anthology includes essays by a wide variety of behavioral scientists and represents a summary of current literature on voluntary associations.*

Goldhammer, Herbert. "Some Factors Affecting Participation in Voluntary Associations." *Contributions to Urban Sociology.* (Edited by E. W. Burgess and D. Bogue.) Chicago: University of Chicago Press, 1964. pp. 224-30. *Surveys some correlates of membership in voluntary associations.*

Hagedorn, Robert, and Labovitz, Sanford. "An Analysis of Community and Professional Participation Among Occupations." *Social Forces* 45:483-91; June 1967. *Study of the correlation of various occupational groups with membership and participation in voluntary associations.*

Hausknecht, Murray. *The Joiners: A Sociological Description of Voluntary Association Membership in the United States.* New York: Bedminster Press, 1962. *Presentation of data from a national survey research study on membership in voluntary associations. Analyzes the validity of traditional theories about the role of voluntary associations in society. Provides a survey of the literature and a full bibliography.*

Hoffer, Joe R. "Adult Education in Voluntary Social Welfare Organizations." *Handbook of Adult Education in the United States.* (Edited by Malcolm Knowles.) Chicago: Adult Education Association, 1960. pp. 366-77. *Focuses on the influence of experiences in social welfare organizations on the learning process of adults. Such experiences may be seen as part of an informal adult education process.*

Komarovsky, Mirra. "The Voluntary Associations of Urban Dwellers." *American Sociological Review* 11:686-98; December 1946. *Classic study of the memberships that city dwellers hold in voluntary associations.*

Levitte, Mendel. "Adult Education Through Voluntary Health Agencies." *Handbook of Adult Education in the United States.*

(Edited by Malcolm Knowles.) Chicago: Adult Education Association, 1960. pp. 255-62. *Discussion of the role played by voluntary health organizations in adult education.*

Merrifield, Charles W., editor. *Leadership in Voluntary Enterprise.* Council of National Organizations for Adult Education. New York: Oceana Publications, 1961. *Anthology of philosophical and analytical essays on leadership, structure, and role of voluntary organizations.*

Morris, Raymond M. N. "British and American Research on Voluntary Associations: A Comparison." *Sociological Inquiry* 35: 186-200; 1965. *Reviews the British and American literature on voluntary associations with an eye to the differences in approach, emphasis, and subject.*

National Health Council. *Voluntarism and Health: The Role of the National Voluntary Health Agency.* New York: the Council, 1962. *A history of voluntary health agencies and a projection of the future of voluntarism in health.*

National Social Welfare Assembly. *The Role of Voluntary Social Welfare Agencies: A Report.* New York: the Assembly, 1961. *Focuses primarily on problems and potentials of voluntary organizations. One section deals with the relationship of staff and volunteers.*

Palisi, Bartolomeo J. "A Critical Analysis of the Voluntary Association Concept." *Sociology and Social Research* 52:392-405; July 1968. *Theoretical consideration of the concept of the voluntary association and the social conditions that influence its form and membership. Attempts to draw implications for research.*

Sills, David L. *The Volunteers: Means and Ends in a National Organization.* Glencoe, Illinois: Free Press, 1957. *Based on an intensive study of the National Foundation for Infantile Paralysis, which is highly successful in recruitment and use of volunteers. Focuses on the organization's characteristics and on the motivations of its volunteers.*

Smith, Clagett G., and Tannenbaum, Arnold S. "Some Implications of Leadership and Control for Effectiveness in a Voluntary Association." *Human Relations* 18:265-72; August 1965. *Studies the results of officers' leadership characteristics on the effectiveness of the League of Women Voters.*

Smith, Constance, Freedman, Anne. *Voluntary Associations: Perspectives in Literature.* Harvard University Press, Cambridge, 1972. *This is a survey of the literature on voluntary associations with an annotated bibliography of over 600 items.*

Smith, David Horton. "The Importance of Formal Voluntary Organization for Society." *Sociology and Social Research* 50:483-94; July 1966. *Scholarly analysis of the functions voluntary organizations perform in the social system.*

Smith, David-Horton, Schultz, Marge; Marsh, Barbara; Orme, Cathy. *General Voluntarism: Annotated Bibliography 1973.* Center for a Voluntary Society, Washington, D.C., 1973.

Warriner, Charles K., and Prather, Jane Emery. "Four Types of Voluntary Associations." *Sociological Inquiry* 35:138-48; April 1965. *A classificatory scheme which analyzes 35 voluntary associations and groups them into four types according to the functions they fulfill. Each type is found to have different organizational characteristics and kinds of activity.*

VI. Resource Inventories

A. Bibliographies

Adams, Ethel M., and Cope, Suzanne D. *Volunteers: An Annotated Bibliography.* New York: United Community Funds and Councils of America, 1968. *Extensive classified bibliography covering most aspects of the field.*

Arffa, Marvin S. *High School and College Student Volunteers in Community and Psychiatric Settings: A Bibliography with Selected Annotations.* Supplementary mailing. Washington, D.C.: American Psychiatric Association, Mental Health Service, 1966. *Very extensive list of citations for this specialized group of volunteers.*

Johnson, Guion Griffis. *Volunteers in Community Service.* North Carolina Council of Women's Organizations, Chapel Hill, North Carolina. Durham: Seeman Printery, 1967. *Reports an intensive study of North Carolina volunteers and volunteer supervisors. Includes extensive bibliography with special focus on the role of volunteers in fighting poverty.*

Kroeger, Naomi. "Role of the Volunteer in Contemporary Society: A Survey of the Literature." *100,000 Hours a Week: Volunteers in Service to Youth and Families.* New York: National Federation of Settlements and Neighborhood Centers, 1965. pp. 75-84. *Summarizes the content of literature in the field; does not cite actual titles.*

National Social Welfare Assembly. *Some New Material on Volunteers.* New York: the Assembly, 1966. *Brief survey of recent materials, grouped primarily according to the volunteer work setting.*

Scheier, Ivan H. *Volunteer Programs in Courts: Collected Papers on Productive Programs.* U.S. Department of Health, Education, and Welfare, Social and Rehabilitation Service, Office of Juvenile Delinquency and Youth Development. Washington, D.C.: the Department, 1969. *Extensive bibliography lists relevant directories, films, tapes, and newsletters, as well as books and articles.*

U.S. Department of the Army. *The Volunteer: An Annotated Bibliography for Use in Army Community Service.* Pamphlet No. 608-25. Washington, D.C.: the Department, 1967. *Lengthy annotations in a bibliography divided into a wide variety of categories. Draws heavily from material on civilian volunteer programs.*

B. Periodicals Dealing Primarily with Volunteers

Voluntary Action News, published bi-monthly by the National Center for Voluntary Action, Washington, D.C. *This is an up to date newsletter about volunteers and voluntarism available to subscribers by writing to NCVA.*

Volunteer Administration. Quarterly. Boston: Northeastern University. *Deals with issues of administration and supervision of volunteer programs. Offers articles and materials keyed to the development and coordination of such programs.*

Volunteer Leader (before 1969 entitled *The Auxiliary Leader*). Monthly journal for hospital auxiliaries. Chicago: American Hospital Association. *Provides articles and exchange of news and tips for volunteers in hospital settings, many of them members of hospital auxiliaries.*

Volunteer Viewpoint. Monthly newsletter of the American Volunteer Bureaus. New York: United Community Funds and Councils of America. *Deals with people and programs, studies, and resource materials for and about volunteers.*

Volunteer's Digest. Bimonthly. Washington, D.C.: Volunteer Community Activities Clearinghouse. *Ideas and new items in the volunteer field. Notices of current research and new publications.*

C. Listings of Volunteer Opportunities

Commission on Youth Service Projects. *Invest Yourself.* New York: the Commission. Published annually. *Listing of several hundred projects with openings in service roles for high school and college youth.*

Health and Welfare Council of the National Capital Area, Volunteer Services Branch. *A Registry of Community Volunteer Service Opportunities.* Washington, D.C.: the Council, 1968. *Sample of the kind of interagency taxonomy that could be produced by any city.*

National Service Secretariat. *Directory of Service Organizations.* Washington, D.C.: the Secretariat, 1968. *Aimed at college students, this directory gives an introduction to general areas of service, guidelines for getting involved, and a listing of organizations to contact for further information.*

National Social Welfare Assembly. *Youth Takes the Field.* New York: the Assembly, 1962. *Pamphlet aimed at the teen-age audience. Attempts to describe areas where involvement in social service may be sought and to provide practical guidelines for self-assessment regarding such involvement.*

National Student Volunteer Program, Directory of College Student Volunteer Programs: Academic Year 1971/72, 1972/73. Washington, D.C. ACTION, Supt. of Documents, U.S. Government Printing Office.

National High School Volunteers, same source as above.

U.S. Department of Health, Education, and Welfare, Welfare Administration. *Opportunities for Volunteers in Public Welfare Departments.* Welfare Administration Publication No. 21. Washington, D.C.: Government Printing Office, 1967. *Describes a variety of roles available to volunteers in different types of welfare programs across the country.*

D. Research Studies on Volunteers and Volunteering

Arsenian, Seth, and Blumberg, Arthur. "A Deeper Look at Volunteers." *Adult Leadership,* June 1960. pp. 41, 65-66. *Reports sociological and psychological data on a group of YMCA volunteers.*

Bair, John T., and Gallagher, Thomas J. "Volunteering for Extra-Hazardous Duty." *Journal of Applied Psychology* 44:329-31;

1960. *Attempts to discover personality characteristics that differentiate volunteers from nonvolunteers. Examines the effects of various conditions on volunteering.*

Hedges, H.G. "Using Volunteers in Schools." Ontario Institute for Studies in Education. Ontario, Canada, 1972. *This comprehensive study deals with the ducation values volunteers provide for children in the classroom.*

Joint Commission on Correctional Manpower and Training. *Corrections 1968: A Climate of Change.* Washington, D.C.: the Commission, 1968. *Harris and Associates Survey reports on attitudes of correctional workers throughout the nation. Several questions elicit data on workers' attitudes toward volunteers in the corrections field.*

————. *The Public Looks at Crime and Corrections.* Washington, D.C.: the Commission, 1968. *Survey made by Harris and Associates of public attitudes toward the corrections field. Includes two questions on volunteer work in the field.*

Matthes, JoAnn. "Volunteer Participation in Social Welfare Agencies: A Conceptual Framework." Unpublished master's thesis, University of California at Berkeley, 1961. *Examines factors that influence individuals to participate as volunteers, to accept certain roles, and to join certain agencies rather than others.*

Riggs, Margaret M., and Kaess, Walter. "Personality Differences Between Volunteers and Non-Volunteers." *Journal of Psychology* 40:229-45; 1955. *Attempts to examine differences between persons who do and do not volunteer for participation in psychological experiments.*

Standards for Central Volunteer Coordinating Services. United Way of America. Fairfax, Va., 1975. *This is an important new document with suggested minimal standards for organizing, staffing and running a volunteer program.*

Thursz, Daniel. *Volunteer Group Advisors in a National Social Group Work Agency.* D.S.W. dissertation. Washington, D.C.: Catholic University of America Press, 1960. *A descriptive study of individual characteristics, training, and experience of volunteer youth leaders in the B'nai B'rith Youth Organization.*

U.S. Department of Labor, Manpower Administration. *Americans Volunteer.* Washington, D.C.: Government Printing Office, 1969. *Reports results of nationwide survey of volunteers—who they are, what they do and why. Examines possible trends of the future with a particular eye to the possibilities of extending the operative labor force of the country through organized volunteer efforts.*

E. National Volunteer Information Coordination and Referral Services

ACTION
806 Connecticut Ave.
Washington, D.C. 20625

American Assn. of Fund-Raising
 Counsel
500 Fifth Ave.
New York, N.Y. 10036

American Association of Volunteer
 Services Coordinators
18 South Michigan Ave., Rm. 602
Chicago, Ill. 60603

American Council of Voluntary
 Agencies for Foreign Service,
 Inc.
200 Park Ave. So.
New York, N.Y. 10003

American Society of Directors of
 Volunteer Services of the
 American Hospital Assn.
840 No. Lake Shore Dr.
Chicago, Ill. 60611

Association of Voluntary Action
 Scholars
Box G-55 McGuinn Hall
Boston College
Chestnut Hill, Mass. 02167

Association of Volunteer Bureaus
 P.O. Box 125
801 No. Fairfax St.
Alexandria, Va. 22314

Council on Foundations
345 East 46th St.
New York, N.Y. 10017

The National Assembly of
 National Voluntary Health and
 Welfare Associations
345 East 46th St.
New York, N.Y. 10017

National Center for Voluntary
 Action
1785 Massachusetts Ave. N.W.
Washington, D.C. 20036

National Information Center on
 on Volunteerism, Inc.
1221 University Ave.
Boulder, Colo. 80302

National School Volunteer
 Program, Inc.
450 No. Grand Ave., Rm. G-114
Los Angeles, Calif. 90051

United Way
801 No. Fairfax St.
Alexandria, Va. 22314

Volunteers in Probation
A Division of the National Council
 on Crime and Delinquency
200 Washington Square Plaza
Royal Oak, Mich. 48067

ABOUT THE AUTHORS

Drs. Schindler-Rainman and Lippitt have been functioning as a professional team for over ten years. They both enjoy the variety of working with all types of organizations and communities, large and small, and enjoy traveling and working in all regions of the country and abroad.

They share common beliefs about voluntarism, intercultural-interracial pluralism, value awareness, interpersonal sensitivity and humanistic quality of life as core values of democracy.

Both began with applied behavioral science training—Dr. Rainman in Social Work, and Dr. Lippitt in Youth group work. As a team they have pioneered in designs for integrating group dynamics with organizational development, and intergroup relations with community development.

Their work on the development of voluntarism has integrated the theory of democracy, the strategies of development of the "Volunteer Community", and the techniques of training for the leadership of voluntarism in all sectors of the society.

Their other thrust as a team, in collaboration with the late Robert Fox, has been to integrate predictions of the future with images of desired futures, and with realistic planning processes and decreasing the energy loss of problem-centered defeatism.

They are currently working on the extension of effective participative learning experiences through the designing of multi-media learning resources.

Both of the partners carry on their own consulting activities as well as their co-consulting practice. They have found in working with many types of organizations, agencies and communities, that a woman-man team has many advantages, and that their resources are complementory in providing consultation to business, educational and health systems, national voluntary and religious agencies, communities and government agencies. Both are also active volunteers serving on the boards of national voluntary agencies.

Both authors are fellows in the International Association of Applied Social Scientists, and belong to SPSSI and the association of Voluntary Action Scholars.

Pursuing their own interests, Dr. Ronald Lippitt belongs to the American Psychological Association and Dr. Eva Schindler-Rainman to the National Association of Social Workers.

They have authored a variety of publications besides this volume.

Index